AF552534

EMPOWERING PRIMARY TEACHERS

EMPOWERING PRIMARY TEACHERS

Dr. B.S.V. Dutt
M.A., M.Ed., Ph.D
A.P.S.W.R.J. College
Tiruvuru
Krishna District
Andhra Pradesh

And

Dr. Digumarti Bhaskara Rao
M.Sc., M.A., M.A., M.Ed., Ph.D.
R.V.R. College of Education
Guntur 522006
Andhra Pradesh

DISCOVERY PUBLISHING HOUSE
New Delhi

First Published-2001
Reprinted: 2013
ISBN 81-7141-615-2

Published by :
DISCOVERY PUBLISHING HOUSE
4831/24, Ansari Road, Prahlad Street,
Daryaganj, New Delhi-110002 (INDIA)
☎ : 3279245 • Fax : 91-11-3253475
E-mail : dphtemp@indiatimes.com

Printed at: Dynamic printers, Delhi

dedicated

with affection

to

sister

Miss. B.V. Lakshmi

PREFACE

Empowerment of teachers raises the sights of teachers, lowers their defensive barriers, broadens their educational horizons, gives them a sense of pride, ownership and responsibility for their area, and creates a climate in which constant development through initial induction and inservice education, though demanding of its nature, will be seen as normal and necessary.

Considering the importance of teacher empowerment, this study has been undertaken to identify the necessary competencies required by the primary teachers and to develop ways and means to inculcate and nurture the essential competencies in the primary teachers.

The most essential competencies suggested by the teacher educators, primary (inservice) teachers, and trainee (preservice) teachers are: The teacher should (1) realise the relevance and significance of teaching, (2) be ever ready to learn new things, (3) motivate pupils, (4) maintain discipline, (5) be a resourceful person, (6) be hard working, (7) develop easy, original and innovative methods of instruction, (8) be honest and sincere, (9) love his profession, (10) develop moral values in pupils, (11) be friendly with pupils, (12) stimulate, impress and inspire pupils, (13) identify the talents in the pupils, and try to draw them out, (14) know the aims, goals and objectives of the subject, and (15) plan his lesson well. The essential competencies suggested by the sample are: The teacher should (1) evaluate pupils' performance, (2) attend teacher training programmes, (3) cheerful and active, (4) communicate to parents about their children, (5) be aware of and pass on the cultural heritage, (6) be consistent in policy and action, (7) seek co-operation from the society, (8) consider individual differences, (9) encourage activity based learning, (10) possess guidance and counseling skills, (11) be sympathetic, and (12) correlate the subjects of the curriculum.

The techniques found effective in empowering the primary teachers are (1) role-play, (2) modeling, (3) observation, (4) micro-teaching, (5) seminar, (6) discussion, (7) symposium, and (8) brain-storming.

We feel that this study will serve as a model to identify the essential teaching competencies and ways and means of empowering teachers in competencies at various levels of education. The national level institutions such as NCERT, NIEPA, NCTE, AICTE, IMC, UGC, etc., may come forward to draw a profile of teacher competencies and to develop the strategies to empower teachers working at various levels of education—academic, and professional.

We are thankful to Prof. M. Sreerama Murthy, Dr. B.S.V. Dutt, Ms. B.V.Lakshmi, Mr. Krishna Mohan and Mr. Y. Venkata Ramana for their mental and material support in making this research on 'empowering primary teachers' a fruitful one. We are thankful to many more viz., authors, authors, experts, academicians, and preservice and inservice teachers who became the sources of this book.

Let the "quality education for all" become a reality.

Bhaskara Rao
Dutt
Teacher's Day, 2000

CONTENTS

1

INTRODUCTION

Teaching, like other professions before it is currently at a transitional stage and is experiencing a serious occupational crises. Its knowledge base has expanded significantly in the present century, but still there has been lack of clarity in public, in teachers themselves and in ministries of education, in teacher training institutions, regarding the professional identity, teacher empowerment, nature and needs of teacher education, and the academic credibility of educational studies. Teachers themselves are uncertain as to nature of their own occupation. They are unclear as to which category they belong—persons, professionals, trades persons etc. If teachers don't know, what they are, they are unsure of demands others legitively make on them (e.g.. parents) and what demands they can make on others (e.g.. Ministries of Education) and, most important of all, they are unsure of what demands they should make on themselves, Ówing to the lack of clarity, teachers have not developed clear statements for their enterprises. Dewey (1929) argued that "the problem of training teachers become species of a more generic affair—that of training professionals, a theme later taken up by others (A Burke, 1997). If this is the case, then teacher preparation should operate within a clearly thoughtout framework which reflects the professional nature of enterprise. Teacher education, however, is a conspicuous example of practice operating without theory and in many countries is the product of history rather than logic. It can be said, with some justification, that the problem with many current teacher training programmes, both at pre-service and in-service levels, is that they are still training teachers rather than educating professionals.

As long as this confusion lasts, it also acts as an obstacle to moves that might be made towards empowerment of teachers. The urgency of empowerment of teachers is highlighted by strong move, towards de-professionalisation of teachers. In England, Government policies over a five year period have served to reconstruct the teacher as the doer not the thinker, the manager not the scholar, the technician not the intellectual and charged teachers to deliver competency driven, school based, teacher training, thus running the risk of loosing sight of the complexity of both teacher education and teaching/learning processes and disempowering the teacher in the process.

TEACHING PROFESSION AND COMPETENCY

While the Greeks didn't have a word for it, the idea of 'profession' and professional education was already beginning to take shape even at that early stage. The first stage is that of a craftsman or technician who operates by rules of thumb, learns the 'Tricks of the Trade' through apprenticeship, and for whom the criterion of good practice is the pragmatic one of what does or does not work. The second stage is marked by more rational and scientific approach in the search of some general and basic rules/guidelines or theoretical constructs to enlighten diagnosis and guide practice. The third stage is characterised by increased conceptulisation and a growing dependency on other disciplines.

No profession can advance faster than the knowledge base on which it must rely. The advent of the behavioural sciences, extensive developments in educational research, a new thinking in the philosophy of education, has thrown considerable light on and led to significant changes in the practice of teaching and preparation of teachers as competent ones.

The complexity of the education context and of the teaching learning process, growing societal changes, growing instability in family life, effects of both on young students calls for a broader perspective and demands more competent persons to operate adequately therein. The professional person is one who is competent to operate in such a context, has learned to cope with the inherent uncertainties of the area, has the expertise and courage to take critical decisions on the basis of available evidence, and has the technical skills to effectively implement decisions taken or to retrieve the situation if initial solutions prove inappropriate, inadmissible or workable. Such developments in teaching, highlight the need for parameters or competencies within which a professional education should operate and a professional process.

THE STATUS OF TEACHING

Teaching does however, present an interesting and rather peculiar case study in professional development and recognition, especially if one takes account of variations in both developed and developing countries. It would fear then that, while teaching can now legitimately claim to be within the professional arena, not all members of the occupation are professionally competent or can rightfully claim the title 'Professional'. However, all can entertain legitimate aspirations there to be proud of the occupation that they are part of, and challenged by its demands for greater competency because every teacher, if competent or not to do so, whether they are qualified or not, every teacher in every classroom all over the world is making critical decisions about young people every hour of every teaching day and taking action based on the basis of those decisions.

Research indicates that teachers make upto thirty non-trivial work related decisions every hour in a classroom context where an estimated 1,500 interactions may take place between teacher and pupils each day, (Burke, 1992). Decisions are made daily about what is to be taught, what approaches are to be implemented to cater for individual differences, what forms of assessment are to be used, and what rewards and sanctions are to operate.

Such decisions are critically important to the pupils who are directly affected by them and to their parents. If there is any doubt in this regard, one has to simply reflect on the impact of an unfair, unjust decision that a teacher made about oneself or simply observe the effects of even the most 'insignificant' teacher decisions on one's own children, (A. Burke, 1997), Ultimately, teacher decisions impact considerably on the social and economic prospects of a nation. The critical importance of quality basic education to the well-being of countries was highlighted and agreed upon at the World Conference on Education for All at Jomtien in 1990.

In light of the above, what concerns most is the competencies to make such decisions and their ability to implement them. It becomes clear that at both the pre-service and in service levels, it is to prepare teachers to make well-informed decisions, to equip them with the knowledge of the content and the personal and pedagogical skills to implement their decisions effectively, and to develop their ability to evaluate their own work critically. The challenge to Ministries of Education, as teachers become professionally competent, will be to recognise their expertise and the decision making role they actually play, to give them more autonomy and ownership of their area, to place greater trust in them, and to gradually withdraw the tight controls that are usually considered necessary when the teachers are untrained or poorly trained in brief, to empower them.

TEACHER PROFESSIONALISATION AND EMPOWERMENT

Teachers' professionalisation and empowerment implies more trust in teachers and will inevitably involve more freedom for them and more control over their enterprises. "Teacher Empowerment" has been coined as a name for this latter process. The name is in certain respects, unfortunate since it can be perceived by those already in control of and bearing ultimate responsibility for education as a threat to their position of power. The more centralised and authoritarian a system is, the greater this threat appears to be. "Power" and 'Responsibility' should be regarded as correlated terms since the former should imply the latter. For this reason, the French word for 'Empowerment'— 'Responsibilisation' — may be more appropriate in the education context since it is less threatening and stresses the sharing of responsibility rather than power. It may also act as a healthy antidote to 'Power trips' on the part of teachers through emphasizing the fact that a heavy burden of responsibility accompanies, rather envelops power.

The picture of the teacher as an "Empowered" professional person is important in the short-term and in the long-term for the following reasons (A Burke, 1997).

1. It recognises the reality of daily life in classrooms-the fact that each teacher makes critical decisions, and the consequent potential of the teacher' role for good or ill.

2. It provides a vision of where the teaching and teacher education enterprise could/should go and gradually creates scene for withdrawal of unduly tight state control which tend to downgrade and demoralise teachers, and in many instances constrain schools and render them less flexible and effective in meeting pupil and local needs.

3. It presents teaching as a complex area where the knowledge base is incomplete, subject to change, and always open to improvement. Such a view of teaching is an antidote to dogmatism on the part of teachers. It also helps to break down defensive barriers to in-service education on their part (e.g., loss of self esteem as one realises or is made aware of the need for change in one's own teaching). It does this by clarifying and justifying the need for constant updating and skill development on the part of all professionals, including teachers. In this context Lockheed and Verspoor (1991) opined. "Until teaching is seen to require professional growth and responsibility, the effect that in-service workshops have on the behaviour of teachers will be short-lived".

4. It potrays teachers as persons needing initial and ongoing professional development. Trainee and practising teachers should not be prepared simply to perform certain skills in certain prescribed ways but, rather, must

be given the mental tools needed to meet professional tasks in ways that are adaptive, questioning, critical, inventive, creative, and self-reviewing. They must be given "Executive Control" over those skills so that they can use them flexibly in multiple situations".

5. Change, especially rapid change, can lead to anxiety and resentment on the part of teachers. A professional vision of themselves and of their future development could help to counteract resentment and reduce anxiety by providing a rationale which clarifies the nature of and need for change in all professional areas, including teaching.

6. The vision of the teacher as a professional and competent person also helps to eradicate the identity crisis from which teachers in both developed and developing countries tend to suffer. If teachers are perceived as professional persons themselves and are empowered accordingly, they will be more likely to respond well to demands made of them, will be more willing to accept responsibility for school outcomes and will be more aware that the quality of service expected of them is analogous to what they themselves would demand of the professionals who serve their needs (for e.g. doctors).

7. Finally a professional vision of their occupation will motivate teachers effectively by giving them a realistic and justifiable pride in themselves and in their work. From such self-esteem will flow respect for their students.

In brief, teachers empowerment raises the sights of teachers, lowers their defensive barriers, broadens their educational horizons gives them a sense of pride, ownership and responsibility for their area, and creates a climate in which constant development through initial induction and inservice education, though demanding of its nature, will be seen as normal and necessary.

EVIDENCE SUPPORTIVE OF TEACHER EMPOWERMENT

Ministries of education donot teach pupils. Teachers teach pupils and, much of what individual teachers do in their classrooms is beyond any tight supervision or control of either school management or education ministries. Whether some agree or not, therefore, teachers already have substantial power. Research since 1960's however, has fuelled the ongoing debate of 'Teacher Empowerment' and factors that contribute to it.

Research by Coleman, *et. al.*, in the 1960s and early 1970s seemed to indicate that socio-economic status and home background factors, rather than teachers and schools, were the most important determinants of students achievement. (Coleman *et., al.*, 1966).

Teachers were viewed as weak links in the teaching/learing process and efforts were made to circumvent them. To this day, according to Hargreaves (1994), policy makers in England and Wales tend to treat teachers as naughty children in need of strict guidelines while, in the United States, the tendency is to regard them like recovering alcoholics who need strict programming through teacher proof curricula. Such approaches, he says, show scant respect for the professionalism of teachers and ability and duty to exercise discretionary judgement in their day-to-day work.

More recent research has confirmed the critical role that teachers play in the learning process. The realisation has dawned that they hold the key to educational change and effective school improvement, that progress can be made only by working through them rather than by attempting to work around them, and that their impact may be greater in developing rather than in developed countries (Lewin and Lockheed, 1993).

As a result, a simple but revolutionary principle began to take shape and guide policy making in this regard. It was that "effective school learning requires good teaching, and good teaching requires professionals who exercise judgements in constructing the education of their students". Administrators, planners and policy makers ignore this at their peril. In their study of effective schools in developing countries Lewin and Lockheed (1993a) state: "Effective schools appear to require a high degree of school level responsibility and authority (for this reason) a principal emphasis is placed on empowering teachers, students, parents and the community to take responsibility for making education decisions and for the consequences of those decisions".

Further evidence in favour of pursuing the path of teacher empowerment has emanated from both developed and developing countries (A. Burke, 1997). The following examples bear this out (Andrew Burke, 1997).

Research on Inservice Education for Teachers (INSET) indicates that top-down, provider-driven, Cascade models of INSET determination and delivery are ineffective. Further more, if participating teachers donot recognise a need as having sufficient priority for them, activities aimed at meeting that need will be judged irrelevant. Consequently, teacher involvement in the identification of INSET Needs, in the planning of INSET Provision, and in the determination of INSET delivery would seem to be critical determinants of its success. While all educational provision should take place within broad parameters laid down by national governments or Ministries of education, the evidence supports the establishments of funding mechanisms which channel finance directly to schools to enable them 'Buy' the INSET which best meets teachers' needs.

Reports from experiments in teacher autonomy in both India and Columbia and also indicate that releasing teachers, even untrained and very young teachers, from tight controls and ministries of education checking mechanisms pays dividends and facilitates adoption to local circumstances and the meeting of local needs in ways that centrally-controlled approaches have generally failed to do (World Bank, 1990).

Whether born out of research, previous policy failures, necessity, or recognition of the fact that teachers already have power, there is evidence of a new and different attitude developing towards them and a preparedness to place greater responsibility on and trust them.

TEACHERS AND QUALITY OF EDUCATION

The issue of teachers is becoming a priority educational phenomenon and it is no mere platitude to state that good quality education needs good teachers. It is quite difficult to estimate the influence of teachers on the pupils and the role of a teacher in moulding the character of thousands of pupils is tremendous. In Indian thought the teacher is assigned a many splendoured role, he is a guide, purveyor of philosophy and knowledge, one who imparts values of "oughtness". In the acquisition of knowledge, he provides both the concepts and also acts as a conduct, conveying concepts. In another sense, a teacher-Guru is an advanced traveller on the path of knowledge, In fact, man evolves as a human being through learning process with the help of a teacher. If learning is process, the construct for teaching or imparting that skill is the teacher (Dutt, Bhaskara Rao and Swamy, 1997).

Concept → Construct → Goal

(learning) (Teacher) (Knowledge)

The guru is a person who opens the mind of pupil to the divine path of realising Godliness and divinity in every object. That is the reason our ancient upanishads raise him to the level of God—Acharya Devo Bhava.

Owing to so many reasons, best persons are not being attracted to teaching profession. So there is a decline and steep fall of standards in education and also in the general ways of living in people. It is the need of the hour for teachers to undergo self-criticism, to introspect and findout the reasons for this state of affairs and to know how far teachers are responsible for the deplorable state of affairs.

If teachers acquire commitment, dedication, love and other essential competencies, and if they are enabled and empowered to perform multiple tasks in the classroom, school as well as in the community in a genuinely professional manner, then a chain reaction can begin starting with a sound teacher in students in cognitive, affective and psychomotor areas of development.

It is certain that to provide the best education, the best teacher should be necessarily equipped with skills and competencies. This is true especially at the primary level where the role of a teacher becomes limitless and infinite since he inculcates the values and positive attitudes in children. However enlightened may be the aims of education, however up-date the equipment, however efficient the management, unless the teacher is competent, the whole system of education becomes corrupt and collapses gradually. Therefore, it is a matter of common sense that the best way to provide quality education, is to empower teachers with required competencies. The teacher should be properly enlightened, educated through proper training and develop sense of responsibility and love towards his profession and with rapid expansion of primary education both in number and extent, the teacher must come out of teacher educational institutions with great perfection in teaching competencies and allied aspects (Bhaskara Rao, D. And Sambasiva Rao, K.R.S. 1996).

EDUCATION IN ANCIENT INDIA

From the time teaching started to gain recognition as a profession, experts as well as common man began to wonder about the effectiveness of the teachers. The examples of Viswamitra, Drona, Sankara, Buddha are of common knowledge. Whether mythological or historical, both Eastern and Western records strongly suggest that the famous teachers were known to attract a large number of pupils around them and their glory used to be reflected in terms of the achievements of pupils.

It has been documented in our ancient literature that after a period of training the Kshatriya Princes were put to test to ascertain their learning outcomes. If a particular student failed to show mastery of knowledge and competencies, it indeed indicated the failure of both, may be more of the teacher. Thus there is sufficient evidence to believe that teaching or teacher effectiveness has been viewed more in terms of what happens to a learner than what a teacher does. Hence, the final learning outcomes of a pupil was crucial in those days (M.D. Buch 1986).

Thus, there is sufficient evidence to believe that teacher effectiveness has been viewed more in terms of what happens to a learner than what a teacher does. What is crucial is not teacher's act, but the pupils behaviour or learning outcome.

In olden days, and during the 19th century the teacher used to exhibit his skills as best as he could. The reason might be the link between number of students enrolled and his salary. In order to retain those students and thus earn his livelihood, he used to be at his best in teaching and only those people who were "genuinely interested" in teaching and who loved teaching took to the noble task of teaching. Naturally, they used to discharge their duties selflessly, sincerely, and earnestly. The pupils intern seemed to motivate a teacher to play his role as a philosopher, seer and also a humanist.

WHO IS A GURU?

We had in ancient India, given a high status to our teachers, we call the teacher by the word Guru. Today we have confined that word to the limited field of religious initiation. Actually the world Guru has got a wide influence. He is the one who opens the eyes and mind of the child to the world of knowledge. The first guru of the child is the mother, the second guru is the father, the third guru is the teacher at school. These gurus open the mind of the student to the vast world of knowledge, with its two internal dimensions, the secular and the religious. Both are spiritual, according to the unifying vision of our great sages. At some stage, after the mother and father and teacher have done their work, the religious teacher comes in, as the guru, into the life of the knowledge seeker of the *vidyarthi*. It is a continuous spiritual education and growth from the seculiar to the religious. The best and highest guru is one's own pure and trained mind. The great sage Sankaracharya in his *Guru Sthrothram*, which millions in India and, now, in abroad also recite, and which begins with the famous words: Guru Brahma, Guru Vishnu, Gurudevo Maheswara, gives a beautiful exposition of the service rendered by a guru. (Swami Ranganathananda, 1993).

Agnana timirandhasya

Jnananjana Sālakāya.

Caksurulmilitam yana

Tasmai Sri Gurave Namah

Which means "I salute the Guru who opens the eyes of one who is blind the cataract of ignorance, by applying the collyrium of Jnana, or knowledge".

ROLE OF TEACHERS IN THE CHANGING WORLD

The International Commission on Education for the 21st Century in its report to UNESCO discussed the strengthening the role of teachers in a changing world. Four fundamental aspects have been found in discussions. They are:

1. The professionalization of teaching activity is the best long terms policy to get quality teachers.
2. Pre-service, In-service Training should be profoundly modified so as to enable teachers master the whole range of educational strategies.
3. Teachers must lean new information technologies.
4. Teachers should be appreciated not only for their knowledge and purely technical skill, but also for their personal qualities. These will be increasingly considered as indispensable technical requirement for carrying out the profession.

The following are the recommendations made by the International Conference on Education.

RECRUITMENT OF TEACHERS: ATTRACTING THE MOST COMPETENT YOUNG PEOPLE TO TEACHING

1. To undertake actions raising young people awareness of the importance of teaching profession, guiding towards it, through meetings with eminent teachers, public recognition of teachers etc.
2. To offer incentives and scholarships to pupils and students with a strong academic record.
3. To promote gender equality by seeking a better balance of men and women in teaching profession at all levels.

4. To encourage qualified people from other professional fields to teaching and providing them better facilities.
5. To develop and offer intellectuality, challenging programmes for teachers educators.
6. Pre-service training for teachers at all levels helps to.
   a) enable future teachers to master a range of educational strategies to be used in different situation and stages of learning process.
   b) strengthening the place of teaching practice through methods employing observation, discussion, pedagogical research.
   c) developing basic competencies in teachers in improving their critical faculties, becoming knowledgeable on the one hand and transmitting culture, awareness of values on the other.
   d) involvement of other agencies like parents' association, business, workers organisation, ethical and spiritual authorities and the scientific community not only to co-ordinate and consult but should also concern their design, initiation, follow-up and evaluation.
   e) improving the status and working conditions of teachers, particularly material circumstances, salaries and other special benefits, autonomy in taking educational decisions, strengthening of the recruitment of teachers.

GLOBAL CENSUS ON TEACHER EDUCATION

Teacher Education (TE) includes both initial (or pre-service) and in-service teacher education and training. The International Standard Classification of Education (ISCED) specifies that education is an "Organised and sustained communication designed to bring about learning in broad sense, while the term training is reserved for education that is directed mainly towards the acquisition of skills" (UNESCO, 1996).

The global crusade to universalize basic education and improve its quality, and the proliferation of national and international commitments to accelerate the achievement of these goals by the end of the decade, have coincided with a global deterioration of teaching and of teachers' conditions. At the start of this decade (1991). The Second International labour Organisation meeting on the conditions of work of teachers concluded that the situation of teachers had reached an intolerably low point, while drawing attention to the drastic erosion of teachers, working conditions world wide and the massive exodus of qualified and experienced teachers. There is no indication that the situation has improved and on the contrary, evidence indicates that the negative trends have been accentuated over the recent years, (UNESCO, 1996).

Teacher Education (TE) has been a particularly neglected area. TE continues to be given a marginal place in educational policies, generally for behind-interms of budget allocation-school buildings and, more recently, text books. The overall issue -what and how do teachers learn, what do they need and what to learn, which is the best combination of modalities of TE-hasn't been an area of systematic research. The countries over the last few years have aimed at "Introducing improvements" rather than at re-thinking the overall TE model (Hallok, J., 1990).

Standards for the recruitment of Basic Education and Primary Education have been lowered all over the world; at the same time, there is a tendency to reduce the time allocated to both initial and in-service TE. Teachers with less (or poor) general education themselves are being trained in less time that too for the sake of training alone which is mostly mechanical and unimpressive. This is clearly contradictory to the declared objective of improving the quality of basic education. Education reform processes tend to maintain the classical scheme of incorporating teachers when the proposal has already been defined, counting on teachers only as potential trainees and implementors, thus disregarding the importance of teachers, knowledge, experience and active participation in the reform process. The common approach of adapting teachers to the reform proposal, rather than adapting the reform proposal to teachers, is still dominant", (Heneveld, W. and Craig, H, 1995).

Fortunately, there are also positive trends and innovative experiments emerging in various countries. In general, however, such initiatives are recent and still limited in size, and more often linked to in-service rather than to pre-service TE (International Commission on Education, 1996).

The following recommendations were made by the International Commission on Education to improve teacher education (1996).

Delineating a strategy for teacher education efforts

1. Closing the gap between educational objectives and teacher competencies

Achieving education for all and improving the quality of education implies a substantial improvement in the professional status and quality of teachers. The building of the new education and the new teacher role by 21st century calls for integral and urgent measures directed towards reversing the present profile and situation of teachers in all spheres, failing which, the goals set for the end of the century and beyond will remain unachievable.

2. Teachers as Learners

The modern education slogan of focusing on learning underscored by the World Conference on Education for All (Jomtein, Thailand, 1990), needs to be understood as a vindication not only of students but of teachers themselves. Ensuring and improving student learning in school implies, as a prerequisite, ensuring teachers the opportunities and conditions for relevant, permanent and qualitative learning in order for them to be able to face their new expected roles, especially at primary level.

Reviewing cost-effectiveness criteria applied to teacher education

The relationship between teacher knowledge (and TE) and student learning outcomes is not a mechanical one. Many of the factors that are internal in student learning are beyond the control of teachers and exceed their professional knowledge or competence. Teachers' role and actual performance have an impact that goes beyond academic achievement as measured by school tests and grades. Teachers' attitudes and expectations (not necessarily attributable to their professional training) can be more determinant in student learning than their mastery of subject or of pedagogy. All this implies reviewing narrow cost effectiveness criteria applied to TE.

School autonomy implies teacher autonomy

Within the current education centralization thrust, continuous references are made to school autonomy and teacher autonomy. It is important, however, to bear in mind that school autonomy can take place without teacher autonomy. Teacher autonomy implies, essentially professional autonomy, and this requires specific measures.

An integral approach to teacher professional development

It is not possible to isolate TE from the remaining factors that influence teacher competence and development. Professional quality is inseparable from quality of life. In the context of the current low economic, moral and professional incentives offered to teachers today, access to higher levels of knowledge and training often leads and foreseeable leads to better job alternatives. The difficulty in attracting the best candidates and in retaining qualified and experienced teachers results in a high rotation of personal and a continuous starting point for TE efforts around the world. TE must be viewed as part of an integral package of measures aimed at enhancing the teacher profession, and implemented within the frame work of substantial changes in the organisation and culture of the school system as a whole.

Rethinking teacher education

The International Commission on Education for the 21st Century in the report to UNESCO, believes that a rethinking of teacher education is necessary, in order to bring out in future teachers preciously those human and intellectual qualities that will facilitate a fresh approach to teaching.

The new paradigam of TE must take into account issues such as

1) Introducing changes in the general education for future teachers.
2) Ensuring acceptable working and remunerative conditions, so as to make teaching an attractive option and TE a cost- effective investment.
3) Defining new policies and criteria for the selection and recruitment of new teachers.
4) Renovating the TE curriculum (objectives, context, approaches, methods, strategies, techniques, resources, means),
5) Setting up a co-ordinated and systematic information, communication and public opinion effort aimed at the social revaluation of teachers and the teaching profession.
6) Re-thinking the organisational and administrative modalities of TE.

Teachers' basic learning needs

"Teachers must adopt their relationship with learners, switching roles from socoist to accompanist; and shifting the emphasis from dispensing information to helping learners seek, organise and manage knowledge guiding them rather than moulding them " (International Commission on Education, 1996).

From the perspective of the TE curriculum, the critical question that needs to be addressed is, what are teachers' basic learning needs (Knowledge, values, competencies/skills, attitudes) in order to cope with the new profile and role demanded from them? What do teachers need to learn to become learning facilators, flexible orientators, habitual readers, curriculum developers, reflective researchers in the class room, community promoters and organisers, systematizers of their own experience, active members of a study group, critical intellectuals, autonomous professionals?

Some basic principles appear to be important in responding to these questions.

1. Incorporating teachers as active participants in the definition of their own learning needs.
2. Harmonizing school curriculum with TE curriculum.
3. Ensuring an adequate combination of both general (subject) and specialised (Pedagogical) knowledge, covering various areas of teacher competence.
4. Including not only cognitive but also attitudinal and emotional aspects within the TE curriculum. Love, affection, understanding, sensitivity and respect for students and their differences, are points of the quality of education and of the quality of a teacher.
5. Prioritizing the gaps in the basic education of teachers (basic knowledge, skills, values, attitudes).
6. Taking nothing for granted: It has been customary to place demands on teacher competencies taken for granted and, a such, are not (or are only formally) included in TE, such as the capacity to innovative, organising (or participating in) group work, designing and administering homework, adapting the curriculum; test design, evaluation of student learning achievement; promoting parental and community participation; organising play and extra curricular activities. All these require and involve specialised knowledge and skills that can be learned.
7. Prioritizing certain problem areas of school performance such as the teaching and learning or reading and writing, a critical factor in school success or failure; repetition, its factors and consequences; time of instructions and its relationship with student learning; multigrade systems

proper and timely identification of "learning difficulties" (as opposed to teaching difficulties).

Areas of teacher competence

1. Teaching for what?	:	Education objectives and goals; learning as the ultimate purpose of teaching.
2. Whom to teach?	:	Getting to know the students, their family, cultural and social background.
3. Where to teach?	:	The class room, the school institution, the teaching learning environment, the community.
4. What to teach?	:	Curriculum content: knowledge skills, values and attitudes.
5. How to teach?	:	Pedagogical competencies in general, and for each subject or area in particular.
6. With what to teach?	:	Means and materials.
7. What and how to evaluate?	:	Competencies to evaluate both teaching and learning.
8. How to improve Teaching and Learning?	:	Competencies to continuously improve practice (Observation, self reflection, self study, research, systematisation, exchange group work, etc.).

PRIMARY EDUCATION

Primary grades, those first years of compulsory primary schooling, can't be defined with world wide precision. In England

and Wales the majority of children in such grades will be taught in infant school (age 5-1 year) and a minority (less than 10%) in first school (age 5-8 years). In the United States, children attend grade or elementary school from age 6 and lower primary will refer to the first three grade years. The picture is even more confusing when an attempt is made to assign exact age to grade for in many countries, and notably in Europe but not the U.K. Substantial numbers of children are required to repeat grades, if attainment is deemed unsatisfactory. Some countries (Denmark, Norway, Swedan, Ireland, UK) rely (almost) totally on automatic promotion, annually; others particularly France and Belgium, make extensive use of grade repetition. Primary schooling starts at 6 years of age in Europe and the United States, at 5 years in the United Kingdom (currently 4+in some cases) and at 8 years, after very efficient kindergarten, in the former Soviet Union.

Broadly speaking, the theory and practice of primary Education in the early grades is dependent upon the streams of ideas, the one resulting from the conglomerate of progressive writings and thoughts in the Rouseau-cum-Romantic tradition, the other founded on the growing body of research in developmental psychology in which right has been pre-eminent. The mingling of different ideologies and theories of child learning has led to much that is commonly accepted in primary practice throughout the world; and as in early childhood education generally, the great international theories of say, Rousseau, Froebel, or Dewey are overlaid with more national or local. In this century, however, one man above all others has contributed so much to prepubertal educational practice as to be cited as the major influence, even by practitioners with only the vaguest of his ideas. This is Jean Piaget (1996-1979), the genetic epistemologist whose serious contributions to psychology and pedagogy lasted from 1919 to the late 1970s. Among the important contributions, Piaget set down perspectives of psychological stages in the growth of cognitive awareness which have become the "leit-matif" of teacher training as well as of half a century of research in cognitive psychology. Piaget sees the adaptation to the physical and social environment as the basis of intelligence and the latter itself develops through clearly related states of thinking. These stages are commonly classified as,

a) Sensory motor, (b) Pre-operational, (c) Concrete operational, (d) Formal, logical operations. For most teachers of the early primary grades it is the third stage which is taken as critical in informing practice since the concrete-operational thinker is capable of much logical mathematical thinking (Piaget's turn) provided he or she has plenty of analogous and experiences to refer to.

The gradual spread of Piaget's ideas during the 1950s and 1960s in Europe, United States, and the United Kingdom was the touchstone of individualised learning and of the attempts to match learning experiences more carefully to the entering chances of the learners.

PRIMARY EDUCATION—THE INDIAN SCENARIO

India's commitment to the spread of knowledge and freedom of thought among its citizens is reflected in its Constitution. The Directive Principle contained in Article 45, enjoins that "the state shall endeavour to provide within a period of ten years from the commencement of this Constitution, free and compulsory education for all children until they complete the age of fourteen years". Moreover, special care of the economic and educational interests of the underprivileged sections, particularly the Scheduled Castes and Scheduled tribes is laid down as an obligation of the stage under Article 46.

In fulfilling these objectives, the role of the teachers must naturally be seminal. Apart from funding and building institutional structures, the diversity and complexity of India requires teachers of special vision and sensitively, if the goals enunciated in the Constitution, are to be fulfilled. In this context, teacher training and the calibre of teachers, teacher competence are of prime importance.

National Policy on Education

Educational policy and progress have been reviewed in the light of the goals of national development and the priorities set from time to time. In 1968 Resolution of National Policy on Education, emphasis on quality improvement and a planned, more equitable expansion of educational facilities was stressed. It was also stated that of all the factors which determine the quality of education, the teacher was undoubtedly the most important. It was on the qualities, educational qualifications and professional competence of the teacher that success of all educational endeavours must, ultimately, depend.

About a decade and a half later, National Policy on Education (NPE-1986) was formulated and further updated in 1992.

Among the distinguishing features of this policy are

* Emphasis on pre-primary education.
* Recommendations to lay down minimum levels of learning for each stage of education.
* Adoption of child attitude, activity based approach.
* Establishment of DIETS for the pre-service, in-service education of primary teachers is envisaged as the cornerstone of educational reconstruction.

In the NPE 1986, improvement in the status and professional competence of teachers is envisaged as the corner stone of educational reconstruction.

In 1990 World Conference on Education for All (EFA) held at Thailand affirmed the will of participating nations including India to meet the basic learning needs of all children, youths and adults. Universalization of Elementary Education (UEE) has been since the priority policy and action areas for the participating countries.

TRAINING AND RECRUITMENT OF TEACHERS

The professional skills of teachers in all categories of institutions except the unrecognised ones are determined by the regulations of the state education departments and examining bodies. The level of professional skill required is fixed in terms of academic and professional qualifications which are taken into consideration, while recruitment. Pre-service Training is organised at levels, i.e, pre-school, elementary and secondary. Pre-school training is given masterly by unaided institutions to prepare teachers for classes nursery and kindergarten. The minimum qualification is 10 or 12 years of schooling. DIETs (District Institute of Education and Training) provide training for these teachers.

Secondary teacher education is offered by secondary colleges of education which are affiliated to different universities. The minimum qualification is graduation basing on the recommendations made by National Policy of Education (1986), the Central and State Governments have made some efforts to empower competencies in teachers at primary level. They are;

1. MLLs (Minimum Levels of Learning).
2. APPEP (Andhra Pradesh Primary Education Project).
3. DPEP (District Primary Education Programme).

Minimum levels of learning

It is a strategy that lays down the learning or achievement outcomes expected from basic education. The strategy expects minimum levels of learning to master upon by pupils from I-V classes both the formal and non-formal streams.

The introduction of MLLs in schools is preceded by

a) An assessment of existing levels of achievement of learning.

b) Definition of relevant MLLs for the time frame within which these can be/should be achieved.

c) An attempt to re-orient teaching practices to become competency based.

d) An introduction of continuous and comprehensive evaluation of student learning.

e) Providing facilities for teachers for improving their skills including providing environment conducive to achievement oriented teaching.

The Central Government is funding 15 agencies to conduct MLL projects in 2000 schools. It is expected to involve around 10,000 teachers and 3.86 lack students.

Andhra Pradesh Primary Education Project

The objective of APPEP is to improve primary schooling. It has two broad based components—teacher training and school building construction. The key pedagogic principle is activity based learning. The programme was launched in 1989.

Impelementation of the project was undertaken primarily at the district and mandal level (23 districts and 1104 mandals in A.P.). Detailed implementation plans are worked out at each district level. Teacher training is organised at cascade basis. District Institute of Education and Training and teacher educators are trained by Project Head Quarters. These in turn train Mandal Trainers who together with DIET staff conduct in-service training to teachers.

The impact of the training is as follows

The project trained 80,000 teachers so far and 10,000 personnel. More than 3000 teacher centres are operational. Lot of differences were found out in the classroom behaviour of both teachers and learners compared to non-project schools. Teachers have been spending time on organising materials or helping children to engage in their own learning. Teachers can develop a new padagogic principles planning skills, assessment, evaluation skills, innovative skills along with specialist skills and assessment of case study research, (Bhaskara Rao, D. 1997).

There are six fundamental principles in APPEP. They are:

1. Providing learning activities (for students).
2. Promoting learning by doing.
3. Developing individual and group work.
4. Recognising individual differences.
5. Using the local environment.
6. Creating an interesting classroom.

District Primary Education Programme (DPEP)

Evolving from the national experience with specific projects is an ambitious nationwide plan to put local communities in charge of their education in their areas and enhance investments in primary Education. Beginning with 46 districts in Eight states, DPEP is expected to cover at least 110 districts by the end of eighth plan period. It has primarily drawn its lessons from and builds on the gains of experiences of the Bihar Education project, Lok Jumbish, Mahila Samkhya, APPEP, Shiksha Karmi Project and Mahila Samkhya Project.

The main thrust under DPEP is

* District level Planning
* Community participation and decentralised management
* Focus on education for girls SCs and STs.
* Improving teacher effectiveness, through training of teachers, improvement of learning materials.

Investments, principally to get qualitiative improvements. This district specific intervention is then backed up by interventions at state level aimed at enhancing the capabilities of state level institutions.

A core group comprising faculty from NCERT and National Institute of Educational Planning and Administration has been formed to facilitate planning at State and District levels. As a first step a five years plan for the district would be chalked out ensuring participation by all major actors in educational system—parents, teachers, educational and administrative, organisations.

Pulse points in DPEP are:

* providing all children an access to primary education,
* recurrent and regular upgrading of teacher competencies,
* reduction of over all drop rate in primary education to less than 10 percent,
* improvement of infrastructural facilities.

Reducing differences in drop out, enrolment and achievement, to 5 per cent between boys and girls and the disadvantaged social groups.

An increase of at 25 per cent in average primary learning achievement levels measured against mark surveys.

India, under the agencies of the Ministry of Human Resource Development, a National Foundation for Teachers has been set up which provides facilities for teachers' welfare. National award for teachers is also a motivational factor for teachers at primary, secondary and higher levels which carries Rs. 10,000/- cash, a silver medal and a merit certificate.

The material which is given under the Introduction section by the researcher may be lengthy but it is quite evident that various educationists like Kothari, A. Burke, (1997), etc. and various national agencies like NCERT, NPE and International Commissions emphasized that there is an urgent need for training the teachers to increase their competency base. International agencies like UNESCO has pointed out various areas of teaching competency and International Commission on Education clearly indicated that the teacher education should be revamped and a new paradigm should be developed to rethink teacher education which includes defining new polices and criteria for selection and recruitment of teachers and identifying the areas of teaching skills relating to curriculum, class room, community, pedagogy and the means and ways of empowerment.

The responsibility and role of a teacher at primary level is more crucial when compared to teachers at higher levels for two reasons. First the primary education has additional responsibilities of providing Education For All and reducing wastage and stagnation in children. Secondly he is the first person in school who inculcates moral values and positive attitudes in children and moreover he moulds the children as worthy citizens in the early years of learning. Training at primary level should be qualitative and at the same time lengthy which alone can improve the quality of basic education. Research by Heneveld, W. and Craig, H. (1995) emphasizes the fact that training for teacher should be meaningful and comprehensive. International Commission on Education (1996) opines that innovative experiments and training to raise the competencies in teachers are still limited in size and often linked to in-service rather than pre-service and clearly indicated that permanent and qualitative learning should be ensured not only for students but also for teachers at primary level.

Moreover, the review of related research (Chapter -II) also reveals the fact that most of the research has been done in areas like teacher competence, teacher effectiveness and personality characteristics of teachers and various factors that influenced teaching but no considerable work has been done and notable contribution has not been made to find out the most essential competencies and the means and methods of empowering them in teachers at primary level through a systematic procedure. Though the CBTE (Competency Based Teacher Education) has defined five types of competency areas—cognitive, performance based, consequence based, affective and exploratory competencies, no significant contribution has been made in direction of developing some means and methods to empower various types of competencies in teachers.

Hence, the researchers felt that some contribution can be made and work can be done in this direction of establishing the essential competencies and empowering them in teachers. The researchers felt that empowering teachers at primary level should be given utmost priority since the achievement level of pupils, enrolment is low at primary level added to the high percentage of wastage and stagnation. The researchers felt that by empowering the competencies in teachers and making them competent they can become better in their profession and can discharge their duties more effectively. Thus a teacher who is motivated to learn various skills and competencies that raises him to a higher level of perfection can also motivate his pupils also enjoy learning and make children believe that learning is a pleasant and joyful experience.

Hence the present problem has been selected and worded as **"Empowering primary teachers with necessary competencies"**. The manner by which it has been worked out is detailed in the following chapters.

2

THE RESEARCH PROBLEM

Statement of the problem, context and significance of the topic operational definitions, review of related literature, objectives of the problem, hypotheses formulated and limitations of the problem are discussed in this chapter to establish clarity and rationality.

STATEMENT OF THE PROBLEM

The topic chosen for the present study is "Empowering Primary Teachers with Necessary Competencies". For clarity and comprehension the meaning of words as have been used are described in the following paragraphs.

CONTEXT AND SIGNIFICANCE OF THE TOPIC

Recognising the enormous potential of education in shaping the personality of future citizens, all progressive societies have committed themselves to the providing quality education for all. They also recognized the significant expansion of higher education and secondary education in this aspect, they can generally be made accessible to only a small section of the society. But primary education can be provided in the present times to practically all members of society with special significance within the larger framework of personnel, social and national development.

In this context, effective teacher education has a crucial role. Infact, it becomes a core condition to ensure high proficiency and quality of school education. In other words, effective school education anticipates effective teacher education. If teachers acquire professional competencies and commitment, and if they are enabled and empowered to perform their multiple tasks in the classroom, school and in the society, they automatically culminate a high quality learning among increasingly more students in cognitive, affective and psychomotor areas of human development.

In the last decades of the 20th century, both school education and society have witnessed unprecedented technological advancements, communication resolutions, periodical reforms of school curriculum, introduction of competency based and value oriented education, adoption of Minimum Levels of Learning (MLL), promoting activity based, and joyful learning, introduction of self-learning and group learning activities, initiatives like Special Orientation Programme of Teachers (SOPT), Promoting Primary and Elementary Education (PROPEL) and host of other developments.

Clearly all these and many other changes occurring in quick succession in school and society, coupled with new challenges to be faced in the initial decades of the twentyfirst century, which marks the dawn of a third millennium, have profound influence on the renewal of curricula content and process of teacher education. If the teacher education has to remain effective, the quality of teachers and allied aspects have to be revamped and renewed urgently, seriously and sincerely. Quality teachers are to be absorbed at all levels especially at primary level and kindergarten level keeping in view the additional responsibilities and special qualities which teachers at that level have to possess. It is difficult to teach for primary level and more difficult at kindergarten level since the mental maturity of pupils is less when compared to other levels i.e., secondary and higher. So, Keeping in view such enormous responsibility and potential expected from a primary school teacher, primary level has to be conceived with a more comprehensive paradigm encompassing a number of inter-related components like pre-service education of a teacher, continuing professional self-learning, recurrent in-service teacher orientation and etc., elements.

Besides providing the quality of school education, the primary teacher has also another task of providing 'Education For All' to children upto the age of 14 years. Educational reformers and researchers planned many schemes for Universalisation of Primary Education. Hence both qualitative and quantitative aspects of education, especially in a densely populated country like India, should get equal emphasis and stress in all endeavours since one can't be compromised at the cost of the other. Hence equal importance has to be given to teacher effectiveness along with the education of children. The problem of shortage of good teachers is to be considered seriously and staunch measures to improve quality of teacher education has to be taken up immediately. This problem though prevalent in all the developing countries, it is taking alarming proportions in India since every attempt to improve the quality of education made by educationists and researchers and also by the government is viewed politically, and as anti-national. Unless there is a strong support from all the political parties, people of all walks of life and officials, no programme can yield good results however, beneficial and sound it is.

First of all, the teachers themselves must rise to the occasion and selflessly strive hard to improve quality of education. Undoubtedly, bringing quality in education is not a simple thing and it cannot be expected overnight. First, teachers should have intrinsic motivation, before they motivate others. That is the reason why the most influential Educational Commission, (1964-66) (Kothari, 1970) opines "the quality, competence and character of teachers to be the most significant factor influencing the quality of education and its contribution to national development". The 1991 teacher training syllabus affirms that the status and quality of teacher education of our country, especially at the elementary level is far from satisfactory. (NCERT, 1991).

Mass expansion of elementary education in India has challenged the State to provide sufficient number of teachers to work in the rapidly expanding network of schools, and to ensure that these teachers are competent (NCERT, 1991). Teacher salaries in India account for nearly 95% of State level allocations to education, a proportion that, in the strained economic circumstances, has almost completely edged out expenditure on other items. Without over estimating the role of education in social transformation, if it is to play its role in improving social mobility and widening choices, the quality and competence of teachers has also far-reaching social implications.

It seems that quality in primary education has been completely neglected and it is evident by the fact that a majority of children in primary schools barely read their own text books even after spending as many as five years of schooling. These children are also not able to attain Minimum Levels of Learning (MLLs) after the completion of the course. These years of schooling are very precious for a child as they infuse a sense of direction to him in the later stages.

Owing to a number of constraints on the part of the Government and other Institutions, teachers recruitment is not being done sincerely. Teaching profession has also become the last refuge of an unemployed graduate because after completion of B.Ed. programme a teacher post is guaranteed. With the rapid expansion of the elementary sector, thousands of teachers are being recruited yearly in primary schools. On the part of candidates who wish to take teaching as a profession, job permanency of the post, decent salary are some attractions. Naturally, these individuals prefer this profession may enter into by chance rather than by service motive. Incompetent teachers thus effect the educational system adversely and become a source of national wastage. So, it is high time to teachers to improve their competency and thus justify their teaching profession. This prompted the investigators to investigate and findout the essential competencies for a teacher and suggesting some ways of empowering them which help him/her to become more competent. This research is a sincere effort to fill the gaps in the already existing knowledge and to add something to it since every attempt in research is only one step nearer to truth.

OPERATIONAL DEFINITIONS

To avoid ambiguity and give a clear picture of the problem, it is necessary to explain each term selected in the title of the problem selected. The meanings of the words have been taken from Oxford Advanced Learners Dictionary, and are explained in brief in the succeeding pages.

Empower

Empower means to enable, authorise, to warrant. This term is now used in the sense of developing and fostering in various journals and reputed books rather than in the sense giving legal authority. Empower thus used in the sense 'inculcate' and to 'develop' in the present study by the researchers.

Primary

First school for children of usually 5-11 years of age. It is also called 'Grammar School' in USA for the children of usually 6-9 years of age.

Teacher

A teacher is a person who imparts or gives instruction, especially in a school.

Necessary

Skills required for efficient teaching and skills required for successful implementation of policies given by the Government from time to time.

Competency

Competency means adequacy and sufficiency. Teacher competencies (plural form of competency) are the skills, knowledge, values which a teacher possess; they are the tools of teaching. Only the teacher who possesses all the skills, knowledge and values can function effectively in a teaching situation and is said to be competent to teach in that situation.

Educational terms often have multiple meanings, different terms may refer to the same concept and the same term to different concepts. So is the competency.

'Competency' ordinarily is defined as 'adequate' for the purpose, suitable or sufficient or as legally qualified, 'admissible', or as capable. The Oxford Advanced Learners Dictionary gives ability, skill, legal authority as synonyms for the word competency.

OBJECTIVES OF THE STUDY

1. To identify the necessary competencies of teachers in general at primary level of education.
2. To identify the most essential competencies in teachers at primary level of education.
3. To develop the means and measures to inculcate and nurture the most essential competencies in teachers at primary level.

REVIEW OF RELATED LITERATURE

The purpose of this sub-section is to enable the researchers to know about some important studies done on the competencies of teachers and to know their teaching effectiveness. The investigators have tried to present as much information as possible to obtain a broader perspective of the problem.

The first recorded study of teacher effectiveness (Kratz, 1896) is one of the earliest pieces of educational research of any kind to appear, set a design precedent that was to be followed for many years.

A large group of elementary school pupils were asked to try to remember to best teacher each of them had encountered and to write down what made that teacher different from others. These descriptions were then collated and composed and from them was derived a list of characteristics that supposedly distinguished the effective from the ineffective for the next half century or so this kind of study was repeated again and again with groups chosen in various ways; sometimes the task was performed by pupils correctly attending edition schools, sometimes by persons considered to be experts, eductors or teacher educators.

Perhaps the most expensive and sophisticated example of this genre was the monumental common wealth teacher training study (Charters and Waples 1929), which used exhaustive and meticulous procedures to produce a number of list of varying length. Typical of the characteristics listed were

1. Adaptability
2. Considerateness
3. Enthusiasm
4. Good Judgement
5. Honesty
6. Magnetism

It is important to bear in mind that at no point in this series of studies was any attempt made to validate any of these characteristics by checking whether pupils taught by teachers perceived as possessing the characteristics did in fact learn more than pupils taught by teachers not perceiving as possessing it at best. The lists described characteristics of teacher who impressed others as the best or most effective teacher. The question whether they were in fact best or most effective was neither asked nor answered.

Two implicit assumptions underlined these studies. One is that just about any one who has ever been to school is a good judge of teacher effectiveness. The other is that good teachers are born, not made.

The first assumption is prevalent even today. It seems to arise from the fact that almost anyone who watches a teacher at work forms immediately an unshakable impression of how effective a teacher is. The basis of these impressions are clear, but they are vivid and the phenomena is universal. The credibility of the approach to the study of the teacher effectiveness used in this research clearly depends on an uncritical acceptance of the assumption that these impressions are correct.

The assumption that teachers are born, not made is implicit in the nature of the characteristics listed, most of which are recognisable as pre-existing teacher characteristics as qualities like honesty, magnetism that is not acquired by taking professional educational courses.

Reudiger and Strayer (1910) found that the personality of teachers was considered to have relatively high correlation with success in teaching.

Boyce (1912) reported that intellectual capacity in best teachers ranked first among the top five factors.

Brokkover (1935) found that teachers' attitude towards work was not related to effectiveness as measured by pupil gains. However teachers who had close relations with students were considered to be better teachers by the students and employers. Also, teachers who enjoyed their work were considered better teachers by superintendents and pupils.

Simon (1936) pointed out that teachers' unsatisfactory adjustment to the community and to the social environment as a reason for the unpopularity of teachers among students. The teaching of such such teachers was not found to be effective.

Hart (1936) examined and studied the high school pupils to list characteristics if they had liked best. The six most frequently found characteristics were.

1. The teacher has teaching skills.
2. Is cheerful and good natured, patient not irritable.
3. Is friendly, compassionable.
4. Interested in pupils, understands them.
5. Is impartial.
6. Fair in grading and marking.

Ellissen and Martin (1940) in summarising their research concluded that

1. Interest in teaching and attitudes towards teaching were factors associated with teaching success.
2. Intelligence is the highest single factor associated with teaching success.

Shannon (1940) found topper group was always significantly ahead of others in academic achievement. The group consisted of one hundred and eleven highly successful educators as judged by authorities.

Seagoe (1945), University of California, in a study using prognostic tests in connection with teaching success as indicated by a rating scale for practice teaching concluded that tests of attitude and interests have little predictive value.

Ryans (1951) concluded that there exists a tendency for teachers with five to nine years of experience to be significantly higher with respect to success criterion scores than those with less or greater amounts.

Carlile and Fuller (1954) in two similar studies found correlations of 0.62 and +0.46 respectively between success in student teaching and college grade points.

W.B. Knox (1957) conducted a descriptive investigation of situational factors that may influence teacher effectiveness. The results showed that a number of environmental factors such as motivation, in-service training programmes, interest and zeal etc. are related to teacher's efficiency.

Heil, *et. al.*, (1960) concluded that well-integrated teachers were most effective with all types of children, were as the weakly integrated teachers were ineffective with everyone except the strivers.

Anand (1961) found that pupils' ranks agreed with qualities like expression, sympathy, loveliness, beauty, etc.

Jayamma (1962) observed that teaching experience, qualifications could add to professional success.

Shamsherry *et. al.* (1964) revealed that organisational factor, morale factor, and personal factor were identified as a crucial importance to teacher effectiveness. They revealed further that

1) As regards success in class, preparation and execution of the lesson, recognition of the individual differences, relating teaching to pupils' needs and helping pupils to

solve the educational and personal problems were given considerable weightage.

2) Intelligence was found to be most important for success in teaching for a teacher.

3) The next important factor was the emotional quality of the teacher and attitude occupied a more important place than interest.

4) Among professional skills, the following are important; skill of maintaining an atmosphere favourable for learning, executing the lesson in an appropriate manner, maintaining pupil-teacher relationship, recognising individual differences, using proper means of communication and instruction and selecting proper teaching aids.

Kulandaievel and Rao (1968) found that in the class, a good teacher, as viewed by students, teaches well, inspires good qualities in students, reteaches a lesson; treats them without any caste prejudice, reprimands them for their follies, tries to reform problem-students.

Gangappa (1969) pointed out that for prompting the mental health of teaches, it is necessary to develop in them a wholesome attitude, professional competence, social efficiency, democratic outlook and good living habits.

Highly visible and hotly debated during the decade of 1970's, the **CBTE** as it is popularly known (Competency Based Teacher Education) reflected general cultural trends in the United States as well as specific educational goals. The CBTE movement is also called PBTE (performance Based Teacher Education) was spawned in the late 1960's supported by grants from federal, private and state sources, landed as the most effective process to prepare teachers, damned as mechanistic approach and employed nominally for several years by over 400 institutions. By the end of the decade, the term itself was less frequently used in teacher education, but the concept pervaded practice.

In **CBTE** greater emphasis has been laid on performance based competencies rather than cognitive based competencies. What the teachers know about teaching seems less important than their ability to teach and bring about a change in the pupils.

Five types of competencies have been defined in competency based teaching They are:

The first -' "cognitive based competencies"- define knowledge and intellectual skills and abilities that are expected of the learner. For e.g., the prospective teacher can list and illustrate five levels of questions.

Secondly, for "performance based competencies" the teacher demonstrates that he or she can do something rather than simply know something. While contingent upon knowledge is competencies that define skills and overt action.

The third class is referred to as "consequence based competencies". To demonstrate competence the person is required to bring about a change in others. Thus, the criterion for success is not what he knows or does but what one can accomplish of teacher's competence, for e.g., is assessed by examining the achievements of pupils being taught.

The fourth type is "affective". These affective competencies, which define expected values and attitudes, tend to resist the specificity and are more difficult to assess than the three types. The teacher values the contribution of all students in a classroom discussion. They are typically embedded in other competency statements. The fifth type, exploratory competency doesn't fit well into the four types, since, the definition of desired learner outcomes is defaulted. Instead, activeness that promise significant learnings are specified. CBTE programmes may require the learner to work 30 hours in a community centre, discuss schooling with the parents, or act as a teacher aid for four weeks. Such activities are exploratory, they provide opportunities for students to learn about teaching, but specific nature of such learning is not defined. The idiosyncratic dispositions and the experiences in the activity largely influence the outcomes. These are also referred to by educators as experience objectives or expressive objectives.

CBTE programmes donot depend on exploratory competencies, but do employ them when peruse outcomes have yet to be explicated.

CBTE advocates pressing for consequence competencies as the most important measure of teacher effectiveness, they rely on the ultimate purpose of schools (pupil learning) as the major rationale for their position. They would hold teachers accountable for pupils achievement but would permit a wide range of teacher actions and teaching strategies.

Performance advocates and points out that there are many intervening variables affecting pupil learning in addition to the competency of a teacher. Because, they have little control over many variables, (home environment, community life, motivation, interest) they cannot be held responsible for controlling or overcoming them. It only advocates, the behaviour or performance of the teacher with respect to previously established standards. It is the major basis for determining competence.

For a physician, for example, competence would not be defined in terms of whether the patient lived or died, but in terms of adequacy of decision making process as the physician diagnosed and prescribed treatment.

Teachers, too, would be expected to demonstrate behaviours known to be generally bring about pupil learning, but wouldn't be held accountable for pupil achievement.

Furst and Hill (1971) reported that Brown *et al,* developed a teacher practices observation record designed to tally behaviours which fall into categories gleaned from philosophical premises of Dewey's experimentalism. Some of the 62 categories include teacher encourages pupil to put his ideas to a rest, teacher has all pupils working at the same task at the same time and teacher encourages pupil to express 'self' freely etc.

Thakur (1976) found that the outstanding positive traits of the teacher as viewed by the pupils were good teaching, kind and pleasing manners, good advice and guidance to pupils, regular and punctual attendance and equal treatment to all. The pupils were in favour of strict discipline and strict administration. The pupils loved to get regular assignments and wanted that they are corrected regularly by teachers. A teacher who did not let down his pupils was loved by all. A teacher who could identify himself with his pupils found his class-teaching easy.

Arora (1978) investigated into the differences between effective and ineffecitive teachers and found that

(i) Age and tenure of service were non-differentiating characteristics.

(ii) Working conditions, distance, time spent on daily traveling, non-teaching duties, give satisfaction to them.

(iii) Teachers didn't differ in-terms of length of service, satisfaction with allotment of teaching subjects, text books, mode of transport used for travelling to school.

(iv) Effective and ineffective teachers differ in job satisfaction.

(v) There was no difference on personal and family circumstances, material status, financial conditions and leisure time activity.

(vi) Effective and ineffective teachers differed in attitude to teaching, teacher-taught relationships, discipline and punishment, teaching aids, homework, and curriculum

(vii) Teachers differed in views regarding the improvement of educational institutions, enhancement of prestige in society, existing teacher training, maintenance of good relationships among members of school staff, better teacher-taught relationships, discipline.

Singh (1979) worked out to find out the relationship of teachers' personality, success in teaching and impact of students behaviour. He found that highly successful teachers were assertive, venture some controlled, emotionally stable and trusting. They also possessed better intellectual capacity and efficiency and has higher creative potential and level of aspiration.

Sharma (1979) studied the development of teacher competencies of B.Ed., students in training colleges. The investigation yielded and five teaching competencies identified were authenticity, integration, innovativeness, attractiveness and pupil behaviour.

Sansawal and Jarial (1979) worked out on personality differences among high and low creative teacher trainees. The high creative group tended to be cheerful, active, talkative, frank, expressive, effervescent and carefree, while, low creative group was restrained, reticent, introspective, sober and dependable.

In a study conducted by researchers in University of California (1979), to find out of the qualities and qualifications of excellent teachers, school administrators and supervisors were also to give why they though some teachers were outstanding. The officials gave a combination of qualities as the reason for their excellence.

(i) Who has those personal qualities of agreeableness, consideration of others, sincerity, and the like, which made one desirable associate.

(ii) Who is professionally interested and competent.

(iii) Who has among other qualities scholarship and culture.

(iv) Who respects and is respected by children and established pupil-teacher relationships.

The study revealed the following observations:

The competencies ranking the highest the study were:

(i) Magnetism : Approachability, cheerfulness, sense of humor, sociability, co-operation, helpfulness, leader-ship, self-confidence, calmness, Breadth of Interests.

(ii) Good Disposition : Appreciativeness, courtesy, tact, sympathy, consideration.

The next highest group are

(i) Enthusiasm : Alertness, Animation, Inspiration

(ii) Attractiveness : Personal Appearance, Adaptability

(iii) Judgement : Discretion, Foresight, Intelligence

(iv) Honesty & Impartiality

(v) Ability to explain clearly.

The third group includes

(i) Scholarship and knowledge of subject.

(ii) Health : Mental/Physical

(iii) Forcefulness : Courage, firmness, decisiveness.

(iv) Promptness : Punctuality, despatch.

Sinha (1980), studied the impact of teacher education programme on teacher competence to perform non-teaching roles as maintaining good interpersonal relationships and doing office work. He found that trained teachers were better than untrained about the aims of lesson, its appropriateness, its organisation, the use of teaching devices, presentation, questioning, use of black board and other teaching aids eliciting students.

Mann (1980) compared the attitude of the successful and unsuccessful teachers towards teaching profession, classroom teaching educational process etc. The research yielded that successful teachers had more healthy attitude towards teaching profession than unsuccessful teachers. Personality characteristics, academic achievement in professional courses were determinants of success.

Mutha (1980) attempted to identify the factors which differentiated effective teachers from ineffective ones. He found that personality variables—ascedance, submission, anxiety, marital adjustments, extroversion, job satisfaction, teaching aptitude, social value, aesthetic values, economic, political values significantly predicted teacher effectiveness.

Mathew (1980) in his study attempted to findout the desirable teaching competency of a Physics teacher. He found that competency of teacher's concern for students, competency of professional perception, competency of using audio-visual aids, competency of giving assignments are some competencies of a Physics teacher.

Bhattacharjee (1981) made an observation to study the effect of integrating a few selected teaching skills upon the teaching competence of B.Ed. students. The study revealed that training for the integration of four selected skills under the summative model introducing a lesson, fluency in questioning, increasing pupil participation and using black board) had contributed to the teaching competence of the experimental group significantly in participation with control group.

Khajuria (1981) in a study to identify typical patterns of classroom verbal behaviour exhibited by successful teachers of language and science found that:

(i) Science teachers' asking questions, giving directions, initiating pupils to talk, sustaining teacher-initiated pupil talk, flexibility were according to normative expectations.

(ii) Language teachers' higher proportion of student talk to teacher talk were found to be normal expectations.

Bhagoliwal (1982) in his study on personality characteristics associated with teaching found that more effective teachers were characterised by overall intellectual level as reflected in their intellectual capacity, intellectual functioning, emphathetic, imaginative functioning, extent of interest, approach to environment and practical commonsense, balanced and healthy approach, and original thinking.

Vyas (1982) identified academic achievement, verbal intelligence and attitude towards teaching as significant predictors of teaching success.

Kaur B. (1983) made a study to explore the dimensions of teacher effectiveness in subjects like Science, English, Hindi, Mathematics and Social sciences at three levels of education separately and to discover the differences, if any in the judgement of teacher effectiveness in the subjects separately. The result revealed that number of factors varied between 14 and 20 for different subjects at different levels. These factors pertained to different congnitive and affective characteristics of teaching, designing of teaching materials, interaction with students etc.

Bailkeri (1983) prepared a Mathematics instructional competence scale to diagnose the weak instructional skills of in-service Maths teacher. He found that the remedial Self Instructional Remedical Micro teaching Course (SIMC) was effective in improving Mathematics general instructional competence of inservice teachers of secondary schools in terms of six instructional skills taken together and each skill independently except the skill of using black board.

Valand (1983) found that components of the innovative proneness scale significantly correlated with teachers personal variables such as age, size, experience, academic qualifications, professional qualifications, mobility, in-service education, reading habits and professional satisfaction.

Malik (1984) found that

(i) Some personality factors were significantly related with teaching success which was positively correlated with intelligence, emotional stability, tender mindedness, suspiciousness, self sufficiency, placidity and relaxedness.

(ii) Successful Science teachers have clarity of goals and their students found less difficulty with class work than the students of unsuccessful Science teachers.

(iii) Teaching success was positively correlated with dimensions of formality, goal directions satisfaction, democracy, diversity and cliquencess.

(iv) Teaching success was negatively correlated with dimensions of friction, difficulty, and disorganisation.

(v) The classroom atmosphere of unsuccessful Science teachers was full of tension, quarreling among students, confusion in class activities, lack of affinity with class work, and there was favouratism.

(vi) Some significant correlation, either positive or negative, was found between class room environment and personality factors.

(vii) Personality, learning environment, concomitants of teaching success (physical environment, democracy, goal direction, satisfaction, formality), age and experience were some of the factor patterns associated with Science teaching.

Chathley (1984) found that there was no significant difference in the quantitative gain scores across subject areas for the skills of fluency, questioning, probing questions, stimulus variation, recognising attending behaviour, Silence and non-verbal clues.

Asthana (1986) defines teaching competence through a systematic conceptual scheme that interrelates all different dimensions of the activity such as performance, knowledge skills, level of degree to sufficiency, intentions, motives or attitudes. Such a holistic conceptualisation of teaching competence provides for a clear understanding of what 'quality' is to be identified in a teacher.

Pillai (1987) found three major criteria in the 'Appraisal of Teacher effectiveness' They are:

(i) The product, or what students learn,

(ii) The process, or what the teacher does, and

(iii) The presage, the partly predictive factor.

Alix Mitchel (1987) shows that the teacher's personality, his appearance, dress and voice his approach and readiness to share the students' thoughts, feelings, aspirations and struggles, his evaluation and guidance, determine the degree of his popularity with students at any time and under any climate. The role of a teacher at any time is helping in the delivery of truth through discussion, definition and relentless pursuit. They are great, popular, enthusiastic, dedicated and ever motivated by the noble mission of instruction and correction of helping their students to help themselves in self-discovery and independent thought and action.

Mohd Iqbal Mato (1988) showed that effective teachers had a significant superiority on the sixteen personality factor questionnaire as compared to ineffective teachers.

(i) Intelligence and brightness,

(ii) Emotional stability and higher ego strength,

(iii) Happy-go-lucky and enthusiastic,

(iv) Conscientious, persistent and moralistic,

(v) Venture some, socially bold,

(vi) Tender-hearted and sensitive,

(vii) Polished and socially aware,

(viii) Self sufficient, resourceful and preparing own decisions (E2), and relaxedness (E4).

Avalos (1991) found that a low general knowledge base of elementary teachers is acknowledged to impact negatively in various ways on their performance, they are less likely to invite questions since they are not sure they will know the answers and not to know is not compatible with the image of the teacher.

Ramakrishna, A. (1992) developed a scale for assessing the essential characteristics of secondary school teachers. In his research findings he established ten characteristics which are essential for a secondary school teacher. They are:

(i) Hard working,

(ii) Scholarly,

(iii) Open minded,

(iv) Professional,

(v) Co-operative,

(vi) Resourceful,

(vii) Leadership,

(viii) Innovative,

(ix) Self-confident,

(x) Sincere.

Ediger, Marlow (1998) listed out some skills for the student teacher or intern to develop. They are:

(i) Interns should have ample knowledge of pupils. The knowledge should include interests, capacities, home background information and purposes of learners in the classroom.

(ii) Diverse methods of teaching including inquiry, deductive, inductive, receptive, convergent means.

(iii) Diagnostic and remedial approaches should be stressed to guide learners to achieve sequential content.

(iv) Critical and creative thinking is emphasised.

(v) Self evaluation by the student teacher/intern is in define to evidence.

(vi) Faculty meetings and workshops to develop the skills in teachers.

He added that there are selected issues inherent in CBTE, one area of concern pertains to how accurately an observer can appraise if a teacher is not achieving a specific competency. It is complex to write selected competencies adequately specific in order to measure if the teacher has attained each competency.

Secondly, appraisal procedures should not to stopped at the point of his given competency in CBTE been or not been attained. Evaluation results should be used as feed back to guide the teacher. Criteria need to be added or deleted within CBTE, as research results bring forth new content in improving the professional training of prospective teachers. Not all competencies can be stated precisely in CBTE selected guidelines will need to remain open ended, such as pupils in ongoing lessons or units of study engaging in problem solving activities.

CBTE may well add to the concept of quality in teacher education programmes. CBTE criteria shouldn't be considered as absolutes. CBTE standards needs to be perceived as being flexible. Continued modification to teacher education programmes need to be in evidence. Flexibility, not finality, in CBTE is most important.

National Council for Teacher Education (1998) identified ten competency categories in teacher education.

(i) Contextual competencies,

(ii) Conceptual competencies,

(iii) Context competencies,

(iv) Transactional competencies,

(v) Competencies related to other educational activities,

(vi) Competencies to develop teaching learning material,

(vii) Evaluation competencies,

(viii) Management competencies,

(ix) Competencies related to working with parents,

(x) Competencies related to working with community and other agencies.

Avalas, Lockheed and Verspoor's (1998) research findings indicated that there was a positive correlation between length of training and quality of teachers. The research was carried out in Gujarat state on elementary teachers. The findings also yielded that apart from its effect on balance of input during training, a low general knowledge base of elementary teachers was acknowledged to impact negatively in various ways on their performance and competencies.

Kumar (1998) interviewed 50 primary teachers across three case study sites, only three really wanted to teach for the others, teacher training was a relatively inexpensive route to a settled and secured life. This situation is by means untypical on a natural scale. This study revealed why most teachers are not competent enough to teach.

Dyer (1998) conducted another study in Gujarat State, Karjan district on elementary teacher regarding teacher competencies. The research findings said that teachers interest is most important thing, secondly they should know what children feel, thirdly they should realise the importance of creating 'loving and child friendly' atmosphere. More than half the teachers expressed pleasure at the opportunity to give others; there was a sense of respect for the job and an awareness to the responsibility attached to teaching young children.

He conducted research on primary school children to study the reasons for not attaining the necessary competencies in Chhota Udepur, Baroda District, Gujarat. The findings showed that there are certain factors which indirectly effect the teachers' competence. They are as follows:

(i) Most teachers who were local, started other activities and engaged themselves in business by running different shops which added to their income. The Govt. job gave them a sense of performance. Hence they didn't have time to spend in school. Naturally it influenced the results in schools.

(ii) Most of the teachers perceived the local socio-economic environment to have negative consequence on students' attendance and performance. "Parents don't take care of children", "Illiteracy of parents cause problems for children", "Parents don't send their children to school because children are also their source of income", "Parents are not aware and don't feel the child should be educated; they are more interested in having the child work", etc.., are the views expressed by the teachers in that district.

Dyer (1998) concluded that so many factors influence the teachers' competency and as long as these factors are not controlled and reduced, teachers' competence may not be improved. Even though teachers are competent, it mayn't yield good results always. The socio-economic conditions, low morale of parents, lack of motivation in children also effect the teachers' skills.

On the basis of the above review of literature, for developing the characteristics that empower the teachers, the following hypotheses have been formulated.

HYPOTHESES

1. A few competencies are necessary to be possessed teachers as viewed commonly by teacher educators, primary teachers and also by the teacher trainees.
2. Some most essential competencies do exist in teachers which are to be considered as an essential requirement for teachers entering teaching profession at primary level of education.
3. It is possible to inculcate the most essential competencies in individuals and empower them to become better teachers.

The above hypotheses have been studied and verified through a well planned programme, the details of which are explained in the next chapter.

LIMITATIONS OF THE PROBLEM

Any research will have some limitations due to time constraint, non-availability of some sources, geographical area, etc., difficulties and factors, however, the limitations for the present study are found as follows.

1. The study is limited to the state of Andhra Pradesh.
2. Social, economic status of the sample is not taken into consideration.
3. Type of management, of the school is also not taken into consideration.

3

RESEARCH DESIGN

The research design, area covered by the investigators, tools developed and used, selection of the sample, development of the opinionnaire, pilot study, finalisation of the opinionnaire and administration of the opinionnaire are given in detail in this chapter.

3. RESEARCH DESIGN

In order to realise the objectives, the researchers have proceeded in the following manner.

1. Preparing a comprehensive list of teacher characteristics in the form of competency statements.
2. Establishing the most essential and essential competencies in teachers as expected and endorsed by teacher educators, primary teachers, and teacher trainees.
3. Identifying and administrating techniques to empower the most essential competencies in teachers.
4. Verifying whether these techniques have empowered the teachers or not.

AREA COVERED BY THE INVESTIGATOR

The researchers covered Mandal Parishad Elementary Schools for collecting the sample of primary teachers covering the districts in Andhra Pradesh. Opinionnaires were sent to various schools by mailing the opinionnaires and also by making contact with the persons directly.

Similarly, the researchers covered DIET (District Institutes of Education and Training) and Colleges of Education to get data from Teacher Educators comprising all the districts of Andhra Pradesh.

In the same way, information was also gathered from Teacher Trainees of various colleges of education in Andhra Pradesh. The person who have completed B.Ed. course, and were pursuing their M.Ed., course are taken as the sample for study.

TOOLS DEVELOPED AND USED

For achieving the first objective 'To identify the necessary competencies to be possessed by teachers in general at primary level of education' and the second objective 'To identify the most essential competencies in teachers at primary level of education', it is essential that some necessary characteristics are to be first identified. For this the researchers have collected information from various sources like review of journals, books and information obtained during review of literature. Then some competencies were listed out from these sources and an opinionnaire was developed by the researchers. Thus, the opinionnaire was developed and used.

SELECTION OF THE SAMPLE

The sample was taken at three levels. The First level comprises teacher educators from District Institutes of Education and Training (DIET) and Colleges of Education. At the Second level Primary Teachers were taken from Mandal Parishad Schools in the State of Andhra Pradesh. They were working as Secondary Grade Assistants teaching at Primary level. At the Third level Teacher trainees were taken from colleges of education through out Andhra Pradesh pursuing their M.Ed. degree.

A total number of 600 opinionnaires were sent to the sample. 200 for teacher educators, 200 for primary teachers and 200 for teacher trainees for the study and the researchers have received

93 opinionnaires from teacher educators, 183 opinionnaires from primary teachers and 92 opinionnaires from teacher trainees duly filled in.

So, the total sample taken is 600 and the researchers received 368 responses from teacher educators, primary teachers and teacher trainees.

DEVELOPMENT OF OPINIONNAIRE

An opinionnaire was developed by the researchers by preparing some teacher characteristics in the form of competency statements. The researchers have developed the opinionnaire by the information found from books, journals and information available during review of literature on teachers characteristics and competencies. So, the opinionnaire developed from these sources has construct and content validity by virtue of its utilisation in the opinionnaire.

The competencies included in the opinionnaire comprise various teacher characteristics, the details of which are given as under:

Teacher competencies sent for experts' opinion. The Teacher

1. should be in intimate contact with students and be friendly with them.
2. should formulate a sound philosophy of life.
3. should realise the significance and relevance of teaching.
4. must avoid indulgence in self-pity and expressions like "I am a mere teacher".
5. should be honest, sincere and responsible.
6. should maintain sound relationships with community people and public in general.
7. should endeavour to respect and take care of environment because he is a part of it.
8. should understand the changing times and the world.

9. should love his profession.
10. should have sense of humour.
11. should teach the importance of tolerance to children and make them practise it in their lives.
12. should be everready to learn new things and thus constantly augment his knowledge base.
13. must have emotional stability.
14. must be patient enough to help the pupils in studies.
15. must use punishment and reward wisely and sparingly.
16. must descend to the level of students to enable them understand concepts better.
17. should keep in view the individual differences of intellect in students and adopt suitable teaching techniques.
18. should know the aim, goal and objectives of teaching the subject.
19. must have the ability to understand the relationship between structure of the subject and its minimum levels of learning to develop the required competencies in pupils.
20. should develop an abiding faith in education.
21. should make students feel homely in school and that they have learnt something useful in their life.
22. should plan his lesson well and know the skills of instructional management.
23. should evaluate students' performance from time to time and give appropriate work for the gifted and remedial work for the substandard.
24. should encourage activity based learning among students.
25. should use local environment and community resources to facilitate better learning among students.

26. should encourage individual and also group work among students depending upon the situation.
27. should motivate pupils and incite interest in them to learn.
28. should possess the skill of a doctor and a logic of a lawyer.
29. should maintain discipline in classroom to facilitate smooth instruction.
30. must attend various teacher training programmes to improve his teaching competencies.
31. should develop leadership qualities among students.
32. should stimulate, impress and inspire students not only by his teaching but his personality also.
33. should have scientific temper.
34. should be prepared to sacrifice his privileges for the sake of his profession when demanded.
35. should know himself, accept himself and be himself.
36. should possess guidance and counselling skills to organise guidance and counselling sessions for the needy and the maladjusted students.
37. should play an ethical role model.
38. must seek co-operation from the society and self-government institutions and ensure their participation to improve the quality of education.
39. should have self-confidence and develop it in students.
40. should respect the rights of children and in turn be respected by them.
41. must take the help of colleagues and the head of the institution to solve problems related to teaching, social discipline and human relations and streamline personal capabilities for effective maintenance of school.

42. must be unprejudiced and treat all students alike.
43. should identify the latent talents and aptitudes in students and try to draw out the best in them.
44. should have verbal communicative as well as the non-verbal.
45. should be aware of our cultural heritage and pass it on to students.
46. should not feel as master of the subject and accept his ignorance.
47. should be a resourceful person.
48. should be hard-working
49. should help students develop their personality.
50. should be cheerful and active.
51. should effectively relate the subject matter in one area to other area of curriculum.
52. should develop easy, original and innovative methods to aid instruction.
53. should communicate pupils' progress in various areas cognitive, affective and psychomotor to parents by conducting meetings with them regularly.
54. should develop moral values among students by giving striking examples from real life situations.
55. must be noble-minded and show extreme generosity in appraising the behaviour motives of children.
56. should be an eager learner and a scholar of the subject.
57. must be sympathetic and understanding in finding a solution to pupils personal and academic problems.
58. must be adaptable to new situations and conditions and change his teaching to accord with the classroom requirements and procedures.

59. must have consistent pattern in action and policy.

60. must have pleasant physical appearance.

61. must have good reasoning and judgement skills.

PILOT STUDY

The purpose of conducting pilot study is to know the defects, errors that occur during the administration of the opinionnaire to the sample and to establish validity to the opinionnaire.

The opinionnaire was sent to experts for careful scrutiny and to establish face validity and to arrive at a consensus. University College Professors, Readers, Lecturers and Principals of Colleges of Education comprise the list of experts. A total number of 50 opinionnaires were sent to 50 experts. The experts were requested to kindly go through the opinionnaire and suggest the improvement of the items and also to delete the inessential items found in the opinionnaire which are not suitable for the study. So, two alternatives 'essential' and 'inessential' were given in the opinionnaire for the use of experts. The researchers received 46 opinionnaires from Professors of University Colleges of Education in India and abroad, Readers from University Colleges of Education and Lecturers and Principals from Colleges of Education in India. The details of the responses received from the experts are given in the table given 3.1.

Table 3.1 Details of the Responses received from the experts

S.No.	Designation of the expert	No. of experts responded
1.	Professors	19
2.	Readers	11
3.	Lecturers/Principals	16
	Total responses received	46

FINALISATION OF THE OPINIONNAIRE

The researchers received 46 opinionnaires duly filled in from the experts with suggestions and critical remarks. The responses of the opinionnaire during the pilot study indicated the following improvements to be made in it. They are as follows.

1. A total number of eleven competencies, i.e., competencies nos. 2,4,8,11,20,28,35,37,40,46 and 56 are to be discarded from the opinionnaire since they are abstract and ambiguous.

In competency no. 2 'sound philosophy of life' is an abstract term which is not applicable to educational context. It should be deleted.

In competency no.4' self-pity was considered to be irrelevant and it should be deleted as it is evident from the term self-confidence used in competencies no. 39 and 9.

In competency no.8 'changing times and the world' are self contradictory and should be deleted.

In competency no. 11 'the experts felt that teaching tolerance to children and making them practise it doesn't make the teacher competent. Also it is irrelevant for the present study.

In competency no.20 'the word abiding faith' should not be used with the word' education'. Rather it should be used with some individual.

Competencies 25 and 26 needed more elaboration by the experts to give a clearer idea of what the researchers intend to convey exactly the meaning. Accordingly the researchers had elaborated them.

In competency no. 28 'skill of a doctor' and 'logic of a lawyer' do not convey the sense properly and donot fit into the present context.

In competency no. 35 'know himself, accept himself, be himself is too philosophical and cannot be quantified and measured.

In competency no. 37 'ethical role model' phrase is redundant as already competencies no. 5, (should be honest, sincere and responsible), competency no. 9 (should love his/her profession) and competency no. 48 (hard working) competency no. 49 (help students develop their personality) convey indirectly the same meaning.

In competency no. 46 the statement is the teacher shouldn't feel as the master of the subject and accept his ignorance, most of the experts felt that it should be removed because, competency no. 12 (should be ever ready to learn new things and constantly augment his /her knowledge base) and competency no. 47 (should be a resourceful person) emphasise that the teacher should be knowledgeable and resourceful on one hand and the statement makes it self-contradictory.

For competency no. 56 (should be an eager learner and a scholar of the subject) is redundant and already competencies no. 12, 30, 47, 43, 48 demand wisdom and knowledge on the part of the teacher.

The experts have also suggested that it is better that the competencies are grouped under some categories like, school related, pupil related, value related etc. to make the study meaningful. As per their suggestions the researchers have grouped the competencies (50) and send the opinionnaire for the experts for establishing validity. The experts remain the same, a total no. of 50 in all for whom the opinionnaire was sent earlier for pilot study.

Apart from it, the other valuable suggestions like using both masculine and feminine gender for the word teacher, i.e., his/her and a few similar grammatical errors to be corrected have also been suggested by the experts.

The researchers have incorporated the suggestions given by the experts and prepared an opinionnaire with 50 essential characteristics. Since the experts have already eliminated the inessential characteristics the researcher have used three alternatives most essential, essential and least essential so that each alternative measures to some extent the competency present in the individual.

The researcher have also corrected some of the grammatical errors and suggestions to use carefully homonyms like and adopt.

Thus, final opinionnaire with a comprehensive list of 50 competencies was prepared for final administration to the sample.

ADMINISTRATION OF THE OPINIONNAIRE

After preparing the opinionnaire data was gathered from 93 teacher educators comprising DIET lecturers and B.Ed. college lecturers.

In the same manner, data was gathered from 183 primary teachers and 92 teacher trainees. The respondents were requested to mark a tick (ü) against any one of the alternatives given for each competency, i.e., most essential, essential and least essential, which they think is most befitting.

Most essential characteristic is the characteristic without which the teacher cannot become a competent person. Essential characteristic is a desirable quality that should be present in a teacher entering teaching profession. Least essential characteristic is present in a teacher to some degree but its absence does not have much impact on the effectiveness of a teacher and doesn't make him/her incompetent.

The three alternatives Most Essential, Essential, Least Essential give the information regarding the degree or intensity of characteristic which is present in the teacher. Since the elimination process of "inessential" characteristics is already done by the researchers abiding by the suggestions of the experts, only essential characteristics of teachers (50 in all) are left, the researcher have taken the three alternatives most essential, essential and least essential. All the 50 characteristics measure to some degree the competency in a teacher. Hence the alternative "inessential" is not taken for consideration by the researchers since it doesn't serve any purpose for the present study. As already mentioned earlier, the researchers grouped the 50 competencies into various groups.

The particulars of grouping the competencies, performed chi-square test, finding out the most essential and essential competencies from the groups, details of the techniques adopted for giving training to the teachers, establishing the validity of the processes, class room observations of the teachers and the scoring procedure, means and methods of empowering the 15 most essential competencies and the final outcome of the research are given in the next chapter.

4

DATA ANALYSIS AND INFERENCES

The particulars of grouping the competencies, performed chisquare test, finding out the most essential competencies from the groups, details of the techniques adopted for giving training to the teachers, establishing the validity of the processes, class room observations of the teachers and the scoring procedure, means and methods of empowering the 15 most essential competencies and the final outcome of the research are given in this chapter.

DISTRIBUTION OF COMPETENCIES UNDER SIX GROUPS

After gathering the data from the respondents, the fifty competencies are grouped under six heads. This grouping was also done by asking experts to group all the fifty competencies under certain heads after going through the explanations provided regarding the groups. Infact, the total number of groups mentioned by the researchers to the experts were eight, viz., School related competencies, Class related competencies, Value related competencies, Pupil related competencies, Community related competencies, Motivational related competencies, Curriculum related competencies, and Leadership role model. However, the experts suggested that motivational related, class related competencies, and leadership role model may be brought into a single group called Managerial related group. Hence, the final number of groups was fixed at six. The details of the grouping of competencies under six groups and the percentage of experts who preferred the competency under the respective group is shown in the table 4.1.

Table 4.1. — Distribution of competencies under six groups

GR No.	Name of The Group	No.of Competencies Opted Under The Group	Details of The Competencies and In The Group	Percentage of Experts Who Opted the Respective Competency
1.	Managerial Competencies	Nineteen	2,7,9,10,12,19,22, 23,24,25,28,29,32, 37,38,40,42,49,50	70.9
2.	School related Competencies	Two	33,43	61.2
3.	Value related Competencies	Seven	3,6,8,36,44,45,48	80.6
4.	Community related Competencies	Four	4,5,21,31	73.2
5.	Pupil related Competencies	Fourteen	1,11,13,14,17,20, 26,27,30,34,35, 39,46,47	85.5
6.	Curriculum related Competencies	Four	15,16,18,41	90.4
Total Competencies		Fifty		

From the above table no. 4. it could be found that out of 50 competencies, nineteen competencies were put under 'managerial related, two under school related competencies, seven under value related competencies, four under community related competencies, fourteen under pupil related competencies, four under curriculum related competencies.

Out of 31 experts 70.9 per cent of experts preferred the above mentioned nineteen competencies under managerial related group, 61.2 per cent experts preferred two competencies under school related group, 80.6 per cent under value related competencies, 73.2 per cent under community related competency group, 85.5 per cent experts opted fourteen competencies under pupil group and 90.4 per cent of experts opted four competencies under curriculum related group.

Grouping was done basing on the percentages of preferences given by the experts. A total number of 50 experts were taken comprising professors, readers and lecturers to whom the opinionnaire for improvement was sent. Out of 50 experts 31 experts responded to the request made by the researchers to kindly place the competencies under different categories given by the researchers.

A brief explanation of six competency groups and the details of competencies which are included in the respective group are given as under:

GROUP I

Managerial related competencies

The concept of management by a teacher has revealed itself to be a complex one, embarrassing a variety of activities occurring before, during and after instruction and even apart from it. Management is considered to be very crucial in terms if effectiveness of instruction and professional success of the teacher. Though primarily directed at the facilitation on instruction, they are also simultaneously aimed at providing an environment to pupils as well as teachers to maximize their performance. It is also directed to improve administrative skills of the teacher regarding effective class room management including development of self, motivating pupils, etc.

The competencies which are included in this group are competencies nos. 2,7,9,10,12,19,22,23,24,25,28,29,32,37,38,40, 42,49 and 50. The details of the competencies which are placed under this group are shown in the table 4.2.

GROUP II

School related competencies

Competencies which help the smooth management of school work put under this category. Teachers need to possess these competencies to perform their tasks meaningfully at the school level to contribute maximally in terms of incidental learning.

Competencies which are placed in this group are nos. 33 and 43. in details of which are shown in the table 4.3. of this chapter.

GROUP III

Value related competencies

Human beings are what they are because, basic values developed over generations guide their course of life. These values are first inculcated in children by mother and father since inculcating of values are as important as intake of food. Next further and later teachers inculcate these values in children. Hence Teacher's own observance of basic values like honesty, sincerity, love, kindness, sympathy, affection will automatically help children accept and internalise them. Inculcation of these values are possible in children only when teachers put them in practice in day-to-day life.

The competencies which are included under this group nos. 3,6,8,36,44,45 and 48 as shown in the table 4.4 in this chapter.

GROUP IV

Community related competencies

Involvement of community apart from parents, is equally essential for effective functioning of school. It can provide various resources, personnel as well as material, to school once they are mobilised, they can contribute significantly to the cause of quality schooling. Teachers inturn can contribute too in constructive work taken up by the community. Once the process begins in right earnest, a strong link between the two; performance and competency in tune with the over all commitment of the teacher develops.

The competencies which are included in this group are nos. 4,5,21 and 31 given in the table 4.5.

GROUP V

Pupil related competencies

A prospective teacher, under pre-service training, is often told that education is paedo-centric in nature and, therefore, a good teacher is one who, rather than imposing teaching, facilitates children's learning, as per the needs of them. Infact, the role of a teacher is that of a facilitator of learning. The teacher while attending a pupil will have to make arrangements to engage other pupils in self-learning, group learning and engage pupils in activity-based work, identifying the talents that are innate in pupils and impressing, inspiring students.

The competencies which are included in this group are nos. 1, 11, 13, 14, 17, 20, 26, 27, 30, 34, 35, 39, 46 and 47 the details fo which are given in the table 4.6.

GROUP VI

Curriculum related competencies

These competencies give mores details about the facts and details of the content of the subjects they teach. They are seldom made aware that each subject has a distinct internal organisation or structure of its own which contains facts and concepts in the curriculum. Curriculum comprises concept which include principles, laws and rules. These are quite significant in teaching-learning process and understanding them helps in knowing the facts in a more meaningful and lasting manner. These include lesson planning skill, developing minimum levels of learning, having a clearcut idea about objectives and goals of teaching the subject. This minimises the content load and emphasises on learning by using concepts for a teacher.

The competencies which are included in this group are nos. 15,16,18 and 41 as given in the table no.4.7 in this chapter.

Since the researchers have given the particulars of the 50 competencies in the tables 4.2, 4.3, 4.4, 4.5, 4.6 and 4.7, the particulars of the 50 competencies have not been given separately in this chapter. However, the comprehensive list of the competencies is given in Appendix A for the use of the reader.

After arranging the competencies under various groups as per the directions of the experts, the frequencies of the respondents who rated each competency as Most Essential, Essential and Least Essential have been taken up at all the three levels, i.e., Teacher Educators (93), Primary Teachers (183), and Teacher Trainees (92).

They are tabulated under six heads—Managerial competencies, School related competencies, Value related competencies, Community related competencies, Pupil related competencies, Curriculum related competencies. The frequencies of the opinions of the respondents and the percentages along with the details of the competencies have been given in the succeeding tables from 4.2 to 4.7. The reason to convert the ordinary frequencies into percentages is, for the sake of calculation of chi-square values easily and secondly, to give the reader a better view of the frequencies in percentages and thus get a better idea on the intensity of options preferred for a particular competency by the respondents.

Table 4.2—Distribution Of Frequencies and Percentages of Preferences For Managerial Related Competencies

Competency number	Total Sample 93 Teacher Educators			183 Primary Teachers			92 Teacher Trainees		
	ME	E	LE	ME	E	LE	ME	E	LE
2	57 (61.0)	29 (31.0)	07 (8.0)	91 (50.0)	87 (47.5)	05 (2.5)	52 (56.5)	32 (34.5)	08 (9.0)
7	30 (32.0)	49 (52.5)	14 (15.5)	41 (22.5)	125 (68.0)	17 (9.5)	63 (68.5)	27 (29.5)	02 (2.0)
9	52 (56.0)	41 (44.0)	0 (0)	108 (59.0)	74 (40.0)	01 (1.0)	48 (52.0)	36 (39.0)	08 (9.0)
10	33 (35.5)	59 (63.5)	01 (1.0)	97 (53.0)	85 (46.0)	01 (1.0)	30 (32.5)	47 (51.0)	15 (16.5)
12	15 (16.0)	66 (71.0)	12 (13.0)	42 (23.0)	112 (61.0)	29 (16.0)	28 (30.5)	42 (45.5)	22 (24.0)
19	31 (33.5)	59 (63.0)	03 (3.5)	83 (45.0)	94 (51.0)	06 (4.0)	33 (36.0)	58 (63.0)	01 (1.0)
22	54 (58.0)	37 (44.0)	02 (2.0)	49 (26.5)	121 (66.0)	13 (7.5)	39 (42.5)	49 (53.0)	04 (4.5)
23	51 (55.0)	41 (44.0)	01 (1.0)	120 (65.5)	61 (33.0)	02 (1.5)	59 (64.0)	30 (32.5)	03 (3.5)
25	41 (44.0)	48 (51.5)	04 (4.5)	82 (45.0)	97 (53.0)	04 (2.0)	30 (32.5)	53 (57.5)	09 (10.0)

24	51 (55.0)	41 (44.0)	01 (1.0)	106 (58.0)	72 (39.5)	05 (2.5)	59 (64.0)	32 (35.0)	01 (1.0)
28	36 (39.0)	49 (52.5)	08 (8.5)	63 (34.5)	104 (57.0)	16 (8.5)	35 (38.0)	44 (48.0)	13 (14.0)
29	22 (23.5)	52 (56.0)	19 (20.5)	45 (24.5)	111 (60.5)	27 (15.0)	19 (20.5)	42 (45.5)	31 (34.0)
32	56 (60.0)	33 (35.5)	04 (4.5)	106 (58.0)	77 (42.0)	0 (0)	44 (48.0)	43 (46.5)	05 (5.5)
37	48 (51.5)	41 (44.0)	04 (4.5)	106 (58.0)	68 (37.0)	09 (05)	40 (43.5)	47 (51.0)	05 (5.5)
38	50 (54.0)	40 (43.0)	03 (3.0)	115 (63.0)	67 (36.5)	01 (0.5)	60 (65.0)	31 (34.0)	01 (1.0)
40	32 (34.5)	58 (62.5)	03 (3.0)	88 (48.0)	93 (51.0)	02 (01)	43 (46.5)	49 (53.5)	0 (0)
42	48 (51.5)	41 (44.0)	04 (4.5)	96 (52.5)	82 (45.0)	05 (2.5)	27 (29.5)	60 (65.0)	5 (5.5)
49	07 (7.5)	49 (52.5)	37 (40.0)	53 (29.0)	88 (48.0)	42 (23.0)	09 (10.0)	33 (36.0)	50 (54.0)
50	45 (48.5)	43 (46.0)	05 (5.5)	96 (52.5)	83 (45.5)	04 (2.0)	60 (65.0)	28 (30.5)	04 (4.5)

Where: ME = Most Essential E = Essential LE = Least Essential

Figures given in brackets show the percentages of the respective frequencies.

Where Competency no.

2 = The teacher should realise the relevance and significance of teaching.

7 = The teacher should have sense of humour.

9 = The teacher should be everready to learn new things and constantly augment his/her knowledge base.

10 = The teacher must have emotional stability.

12 = The teacher must use punishment and reward wisely and sparingly.

19 = The teacher should evaluate students performance from time to time and give appropriate work for the gifted and remedial work for the substandard.

22 = The teacher should use teaching learning material as a means of meaningful interaction between the teacher and the taught and between pupils themselves to make them work independently as well as collectively.

23 = The teacher should motivate pupils and create interest in them to learn.

24 = The teacher should maintain discipline in classroom to facilitate smooth instruction.

25 = The teacher must attend various teacher training programmes and improve his teaching competencies.

28 = The teacher should have scientific temper.

29 = The teacher should be prepared to sacrifice his privileges for the sake of his profession when demanded.

32 = The teacher should have self-confidence and develop it in students.

37 = The teacher should be a resourceful person.

40 = The teacher should be cheerful and active.

42. = The teacher should develop easy, original and innovative methods to aid instruction.

49 = The teacher must have pleasant physical appearance.

50 = The teacher must have good reasoning and judgement skills.

Table 4.3—Distribution of Frequencies and Percentages of Preferences For School Related Competencies

Competency number	Teacher Educators			Primary Teachers			Teacher Trainees		
	ME	E	LE	ME	E	LE	ME	E	LE
33	11.0 (12.0)	60 (64.5)	22 (23.5)	37 (20.0)	125 (68.5)	21 (11.5)	24 (26.0)	37 (40.5)	31 (33.5)
43	20 (21.5)	63 (68.0)	10 (10.5)	74 (41.5)	99 (54.0)	10 (4.5)	35 (38.0)	48 (52.0)	09 (10.0)

Where ME = Most Essential
E = Essential
LE = Least Essential

Figures given in brackets show the percentages of the respective frequencies

Where Competency no.

33 = The teacher must take the help of colleagues and the head of the institution to solve problems related to teaching, social discipline and human relations and streamline personnel capabilities for effective maintenance of school.

43 = The teacher should communicate pupils' progress in various areas—cognitive, affective and psychomotor—to parents by conducting meetings with them regularly.

Table 4.4.—Distribution of Frequencies and Percentages of Preferences for Value Related Competencies

Competency number	Teacher Educators			Primary Teachers			Teacher Trainees		
	ME	E	LE	ME	E	LE	ME	E	LE
3	77 (82.5)	16 (17.5)	0 (0)	142 (77.5)	41 (22.5)	0 (0)	73 (79.5)	19 (20.5)	0 (0)
6	72 (77.5)	21 (22.5)	0 (0)	139 (76.0)	43 (23.5)	01 (0.5)	75 (81.5)	17 (18.5)	0 (0)
8	53 (57.0)	31 (33.0)	09 (10)	122 (66.5)	54 (29.5)	07 (4.0)	33 (36.0)	53 (57.5)	06 (6.5)
36	19 (20.5)	60 (64.5)	14 (15.0)	61 (33.5)	106 (58.0)	16 (8.5)	13 (14.0)	46 (50.0)	33 (36.0)
44	51 (54.5)	40 (43.0)	02 (2.5)	97 (53.0)	83 (45.0)	03 (2.0)	53 (57.5)	37 (40.0)	02 (2.5)
45	17 (18.0)	60 (64.5)	16 (17.5)	63 (34.5)	108 (59.0)	12 (6.5)	13 (14.0)	38 (41.0)	41 (45.0)
48	24 (26.0)	54 (58.0)	15 (16.0)	39 (21.5)	127 (69.5)	17 (9.0)	10 (11.0)	75 (81.5)	07 (7.5)

Where ME = Most Essential
E = Essential
LE = Least Essential

Figures given in brackets show the percentages of the respective frequencies.

Where Competency no.

3 = The teacher must be honest and sincere.

6 = The teacher must love his/her profession

8 = The teacher must be unprejudiced and treat all students alike.

36 = The teacher should be aware of our cultural heritage and pass it on to students.

44 = The teacher should develop moral values in students by giving striking examples from real life situations.

45 = The teacher must be noble minded and show extreme generosity in appraising the behaviour and motives of children.

48 = The teacher must have consistent pattern in action and policy.

Table 4.5—Distribution of Frequencies and Percentages of Preferences for Pupilrelated Competencies

Competency number	Teacher Educators			Primary Teachers			Teacher Trainees		
	ME	E	LE	ME	E	LE	ME	E	LE
1	61 (65.5)	32 (34.5)	0 (0)	131 (71.5)	51 (28.0)	01 (0.5)	52 (56.5)	40 (43.5)	0 (0)
11	28 (30.5)	55 (59.0)	10 (10.5)	57 (31.0)	113 (61.5)	13 (7.5)	40 (43..5)	51 (55.5)	01 (1.0)
13	45 (48.0)	42 (45.0)	06 (7.0)	101 (55.0)	74 (40.5)	08 (4.5)	52 (56.5)	38 (41.0)	02 (2.5)
14	29 (31.0)	52 (56.0)	12 (13.0)	65 (35.5)	108 (59.0)	10 (5.5)	44 (48.0)	48 (52.0)	0 (0)
17	42 (45.0)	33 (35.5)	18 (19.5)	66 (36.0)	101 (55.0)	16 (9.0)	44 (48.0)	43 (46.5)	5 (5.5)
20	28 (30.0)	51 (55.0)	14 (15.0)	75 (41.0)	93 (51.0)	15 (8.0)	29 (31.5)	56 (61.0)	7 (7.5)
26	30 (32.0)	38 (41.0)	25 (27.0)	45 (24.5)	110 (60.0)	28 (15.5)	28 (31.0)	51 (55.0)	13 (14.0)

27	50 (54.0)	40 (43.0)	03 (3.0)	107 (58.5)	69 (38.0)	07 (3.5)	53 (57.5)	37 (40.0)	02 (2.5)
30	28 (30.0)	59 (63.5)	06 (6.5)	69 (38.0)	97 (53.0)	17 (9.0)	16 (17.5)	60 (65.0)	16 (17.5)
34.	53 (57.0)	31 (33.0)	09 (10.0)	104 (57.0)	65 (35.5)	14 (7.5)	62 (67.5)	29 (31.5)	01 (1.0)
35	40 (43.0)	49 (53.0)	04 (4.0)	88 (48.0)	86 (47.0)	09 (5.0)	20 (21.5)	49 (53.5)	23 (25.0)
39	28 (30.0)	60 (64.5)	05 (5.5)	90 (49.0)	87 (47.5)	06 (3.5)	42 (46.0)	50 (54.0)	0 (0)
46	26 (28.0)	59 (64.0)	08 (8.0)	71 (39.0)	104 (57.0)	08 (4.0)	25 (27.0)	61 (66.5)	06 (6.5)
47	28 (30.0)	53 (57.0)	12 (13.0)	59 (32.0)	114 (62.0)	10 (6.0)	15 (16.5)	28 (30.5)	49 (53.0)

Where ME = Most Essential

E = Essential

LE = Least Essential

Figures given in brackets show the percentages of the respective frequencies.

Where competency no.

1	=	The teacher should be in intimate contact with students and be friendly with them
11	=	The teacher must be patient enough to help the students in studies.
13	=	The teacher must descend down to the level of students to make them understand concepts better.
14	=	The teacher should keep in view the individual differences of intellect children and adopt suitable teaching techniques.
17	=	The teacher should make students feel homely in school and that they have learnt something useful for their life.
20.	=	The teacher should encourage activity-based learning among children.
26.	=	The teacher should develop leadership qualities in students.
27.	=	The teacher should stimulate, impress and inspire students not only by his teaching but by his personality also.
30.	=	The teacher should possess guidance and counselling skills to organise guidance and counselling sessions for the needy and maladjusted students.
34	=	The teacher should identify the latent talents and aptitudes in students and try to draw out the best in them.
35.	=	The teacher must have verbal communication skills as well as the non-verbal.
39	=	The teacher should help students develop their personalty.
46	=	The teacher must be sympathetic and understanding in finding a solution to pupils' personal and academic problems.
47.	=	The teacher must be adaptable to new situations and conditions and change his teaching to accord with the classroom requirements and procedures.

Table 4.6—Distribution of Frequencies and Percentages of Preferences for Community Related Competencies

Competency number	Teacher Educators			Primary Teachers			Teacher Trainees		
	ME	E	LE	ME	E	LE	ME	E	LE
4	32 (34.5)	55 (59.0)	06 (6.5)	88 (48.0)	90 (49.0)	5 (3.0)	38 (41.0)	43 (46.5)	11 (12.5)
5	18 (19.0)	55 (59.0)	20 (22.0)	59 (32.0)	106 (58.0)	18 (10.0)	26 (28.0)	31 (33.5)	35 (38.5)
21	20 (21.5)	51 (55.0)	22 (23.5)	80 (44.0)	87 (47.5)	16 (8.5)	17 (18.5)	56 (61.0)	19 (20.5)
31	39 (42.0)	47 (50.5)	07 (7.5)	73 (40.0)	104 (57.0)	06 (3.0)	22 (24.0)	47 (51.0)	23 (25.0)

Where ME = Most Essential

E = Essential

LE = Least Essential

Figures given in brackets show the percentages of the respective frequencies.

Where competency no.

4 = The teacher should maintain sound relationship with community and public in general.

5 = The teacher should endeavour to respect and take care of environment because, he/she is a part of it.

21 = The teacher should identify and use environmental resources for organising different teaching-learning activities according to priorities laid down for optimum utilisation at individual and at institutional level.

31 = The teacher must seek co-operation from the society and self-government institutions and ensure their participation to improve the quality of education

Table 4.7—Distribution of Frequencies and Percentages of Preferences for curriculum Related Competencies

Competency number	Teacher Educators			Primary Teachers			Teacher Trainees		
	ME	E	LE	ME	E	LE	ME	E	LE
15	60 (64.5)	32 (34.5)	01 (1.0)	105 (57.5)	75 (41.8)	03 (1.5)	60 (65.0)	32 935.0)	0 (0)
16	37 (40.0)	45 (48.5)	11 (11.5)	79 (43.0)	98 (53.5)	06 (3.5)	29 (31.5)	55 (60.0)	08 (8.5)
18	64 (69.0)	28 (30.0)	01 (1.0)	115 (63.0)	60 (33.0)	08 (4.0)	59 (64.0)	32 (35.0)	01 (1.0)
41	16 (17.0)	65 (70.0)	12 (13.0)	66 (36.0)	10 (54.5)	17 (9.5)	23 (25.0)	61 (66.5)	08 (8.5)

Where ME = Most Essential
E = Essential
LE = Least Essential

Figures given in brackets show the percentages of the respective frequencies.

Where competency no.

15 = The teacher should know the aims, goal and the objectives of teaching the subject.

16 = The teacher must have the ability to understand the relationship between structure of the subject and its minimum levels of learning to develop the required competencies in students.

18 = The teacher should plan his/her lesson well and know the skills of instructional management.

41 = The teacher should effectively relate the subject matter in one area to other areas of the curriculum.

PERFORMING CHI-SQUARE TEST FOR THE SAMPLE FOR SIX GROUPS

'Chi' is the Greek letter corresponding to the English letter X. It is written as X^2 and pronounced as kai-square. The statistics, which is used for several purposes. It is a non-parametric statistic because it involves no assumption regarding the normality of distribution or homogeneity of the variances. For this reason, Guildord (1956) called it the "General-Purpose statistic". Hence the investigators used chi-square to know whether equal probability hypothesis is tenable or not. That is, the difference in the frequencies opted by respondents as most essential, essential and least essential is due to chance or real. So, the researchers performed chi-square test for the sample for six groups. The details are shown in Tables 4.9 to 4.14.

When the data are expressed in terms of frequencies or proportions or percentages, a chi-square test is used. Though, the chi-square is generally applied to discrete data, any continuous data can be reduced to the categories in such a way that they can be treated as discrete data and then, the application of chi-square can be justified. The formula for calculating chi-square is as under.

$$X^2 = \sum \frac{(fo-fe)^2}{fe}$$

Where X^2 is chi-square.

fo = observed frequency

fe = expected or theoretical frequency.

For each category, there will be a fo (observed frequency). The fo's are measured measures, measures made on nominal scale, i.e., by counting. Then for each fo, we find out the corresponding expected or theoretical frequency. Expected frequencies are frequencies under various categories when the two variables are not associated. Then, we find out the difference between fo and fe (expected frequency) for each category in the table. Then we also find (fo-fe). This square difference, when divided by fe gives the chi-square value.

To be more precise for example, 100 students answer to an item in an attitude scale. The item has five categories of response options—strongly agree, agree, neutral, disagree, strongly disagree. According to equal probability hypothesis, the expected or theoretical frequency of responses given by 100 students would be 20 in each. The Chi-square would test whether or not equal probability hypothesis is tenable. If the value of the chi-square test is significant, the equal probability hypothesis becomes tenable. So, it is used to last the goodness of fit between two distributions.

The scores (actual frequencies) were converted to percentages by the researchers so that basing on equal probability hypothesis the expected frequency of responses given by teacher eductors, primary teachers and teacher trainees would be 33.33, since there are three alternatives most essential, essential and least essential.

The expected frequency fe is $\frac{100}{3}$ = 33.3, basing on the assumption that the number of respondents in each category is 100. The researchers have converted actual frequencies of the responses of the sample into percentages and then carried out the chi-square test using the percentages. Though it is customary to perform the chi-square test using actual scores, the researchers have taken the percentages instead of the actual scores so that, a uniform of expected frequency (fe) of 33.3 can be maintained while carrying out the statistical work. The researchers have shown performing chi-square from the table 4.9 under managerial related competency group as an example for competency no. 25 it is as follows in the table 4.8.

The chi-square values are calculated using the formula

$$X^2 = \Sigma \frac{(fo-fe)^2}{fe}$$

where X^2 = Chi-square
fo = frequency observed
fe = frequency expected

Table 4.8—Performing chi-square test for a frequency

Alternatives Frequencies	ME	E	LE
fo =	44	51.5	4.5
fe =	33.3	33.3	33.3

where fo = Frequency Observed
fe = Frequency Expected
ME = Most Essential
E = Essential
L = Least Essential

$$X^2 = \frac{(44-33.3)^2}{33.3} + \frac{(51.5-33.3)^2}{33.3} + \frac{(4.5-33.3)^2}{33.3}$$

$$= \frac{(10.7)^2}{33.3} + \frac{(18.2)^2}{33.3} + \frac{(-28.8)^2}{33.3}$$

$$= \frac{114.49}{33.3} + \frac{331.24}{33.3} + \frac{829.44}{33.3}$$

$$= \frac{1275.17}{33.3}$$

$= 38.29$

$= 38.30$ (corrected to nearest decimal)

Similarly, for the same competency no. 25 the chi-square value in primary teachers category is 45.20 and teacher trainees category it is 33.90.

Degrees of Freedom (DF)

Degrees of freedom is the extent to which one can have the freedom to change the values of a variable under the given conditions. In statistical language it can be said that the degree of freedom is the number of observations that are independent of each other. The degree of freedom is calculated using the formula (r-1)(c-1) where r denotes the number of rows and c denotes the number of columns. For the above statistic the number of rows are 2 (fo and fe) and the number of columns are 3 (most essential, essential and least essential). Hence, using the formula (r-1)c-1) it is (2-1)(3-1) which is 2. So, the degree of freedom (df) is fixed at 2.

The table value for chi-square at df(2) at 0.05 level is 5.991 and at 0.01 level it is 9.210. The chi-square values for competency no.25 in teacher educators category is 38.3 and in primary teachers category, it is 45.2 and in teacher trainees, it is 33.9. The calculated valued 38.3, 45.2 and 33.9, all exceed the table values 5.991 at 0.05 level and 9.210 at 0.01 level.

Hence, the chi-square values indicate tell that there is a specific tendency for a particular option and there is no chance factor. Similarly for all the other competencies under the six groups the chi-square values have been calculated for teacher educators, primary teachers and teacher trainees following the same procedure explained above and the chi-square values were verified with the table values at 0.05 and 0.01 levels at df(2). Thus the chi-square values which exceed the table values at df(2) and found to be significant at 0.05 and 0.01 levels. The values which are less when compared to the table values are found to be non-significant (N.S) and are discarded.

After verifying the chi-square values calculated by the researcher and comparing with the table values for the competency no.33 from table no. 4.10. under school related competency it has been found that the chi-square value of 3.2 in the teacher trainee's category is not significant at 0.05 level and 0.01 level. It is hence discarded for consideration even though it is found significant at 0.01 level in other two categories, teacher educators and primary teachers with chi-square values of 45.7 and 56.8 respectively because researchers have to establish the most essential competencies commonly desired by teacher educators, primary teachers and teacher trainees.

In the same way competency no.5 in the table 4.12 under community related competency group in the teacher trainee category has a chi-square value of 1.6 which is not significant at 0.05 level, hence discarded. Similarly competency no.26 in the table 4.13 under pupil related competency group in the teacher educators category has a chi-square value of 3.02 which is also not significant at 0.05 level, hence discarded. So, a total no.of

3 competencies out of 50 were discarded for consideration for the present study. They are given as under.

Competency No.		Name of the Competency
5	—	The teacher should endeavour to respect and take care of environment because he is a part of it.
26	—	The teacher should develop leadership qualities among students.
33	—	The teacher should ensure participation from colleagues and the Head of the Institution to solve problems related to teachers, social discipline and human relations and streamline personnel capabilities for effective maintenance of school.

The details of the distribution of chi-square values for the six groups managerial related, school related, value related, community related, pupil related and curriculum related for the three categories, i.e. teacher educators, primary teachers and teacher trainees are shown in the tables 4.9, 4.10, 4.11, 4.12, 4.13, 4.14 respectively in the following pages.

Table 4.9—Distribution of chi-square values for managerial related competency group

Competency number	Teacher Educators					Primary Teachers					Teacher Trainees				
	ME	E	LE	CHI-Square Value	Level of Significance	ME	E	LE	CHI-Square Value	Level of Significance	ME	E	LE	CHI-Square Value	Level of Significance
2	61.0	31.0	8.0	42.4	0.01	50.0	47.5	2.5	42.9	0.01	56.5	34.5	9.0	33.9	0.01
7	32.0	52.5	15.5	20.6	0.01	22.5	68.0	9.5	56.6	0.01	68.5	29.5	2.0	67.0	0.01
9	56.0	44.0	0	52.2	0.01	59.0	40.0	0.5	53.4	0.01	52.0	39.0	9.0	29.2	0.01
10	35.5	63.5	1.0	58.8	0.01	53.0	46.5	0.5	49.2	0.01	32.5	51.0	16.5	17.9	0.01
12	16.0	71.0	13.0	64.0	0.01	23.0	61.0	16.0	35.2	0.01	30.5	45.5	24.0	7.3	0.05
19	33.5	63.0	3.5	53.1	0.01	45.0	51.0	4.0	39.3	0.01	36.0	63.0	1.0	58.0	0.01
22	58.0	40.0	2.0	49.1	0.01	26.5	66.0	7.5	53.5	0.01	42.5	53.0	4.5	39.1	0.01
23	55.0	44.0	1.0	48.9	0.01	65.5	33.0	1.0	61.5	0.01	64.0	32.5	3.5	55.0	0.01
24	55.0	44.0	1.0	48.9	0.01	58.0	39.5	2.5	47.9	0.01	64.0	35.0	1.0	59.7	0.01
25	44.0	51.5	4.5	38.3	0.01	45.0	53.0	2.0	45.2	0.01	32.5	57.5	10.0	33.9	0.01
28	39.0	52.5	8.5	30.5	0.01	34.5	57.0	8.5	35.5	0.01	38.0	48.0	14.0	18.3	0.01

29	23.5	56.0	20.5	18.8	0.01	24.5	60.5	15.0	34.6	0.01	20.5	45.5	34.0	9.4	0.01
32	60.0	35.5	4.5	46.5	0.01	58.0	42.0	0	54.0	0.01	48.0	46.5	5.5	34.7	0.01
37	51.5	44.0	4.5	38.3	0.01	58.0	37.5	5.0	42.8	0.01	51.0	43.5	5.5	35.7	0.01
38	54.0	43.0	3.0	43.3	0.01	63.0	36.5	0.5	59.1	0.01	65.0	34.0	1.0	61.5	0.01
40	34.0	62.5	3.0	51.4	0.01	48.0	51.0	1.0	47.2	0.01	46.5	53.5	0	50.2	0.01
42	51.5	44.0	4.5	38.3	0.01	52.5	45.0	2.5	43.7	0.01	65.0	29.5	5.5	53.8	0.01
49	7.5	52.5	40.0	32.4	0.01	29.0	48.0	23.0	10.2	0.01	10.0	36.0	54.0	29.4	0.01
50	48.5	46.0	5.5	34.9	0.01	52.5	45.5	2.0	44.9	0.01	65.0	30.5	4.5	55.3	0.01

for df (2) Chi-square value at 0.01 level is 9.210 and at 0.05 level it is 5.991

ME = Most Essential

E = Essential

LE = Least Essential

Table 4.10—Distribution of chi-square values for school related competency group

Competency number	Teacher Educators					Primary Teachers					Teacher Trainees				
	ME	E	LE	CHI-Square Value	Level of Significance	ME	E	LE	CHI-Square Value	Level of Significance	ME	E	LE	CHI-Square Value	Level of Significance
33*	12.0	64.5	23.5	45.7	0.01	20.0	68.5	11.5	56.8	0.01	26.0	40.5	33.5	3.2	N.S.
43	21.5	68.0	10.5	55.9	0.01	41.5	54.0	4.5	39.7	0.01	38.0	52.0	10.0	27.5	0.01

for df(2) Chi-square value at 0.01 level is 9.210 and at 0.05 level is is 5.991

N.S = Non Significant *indicates that the competency is discarded.

ME = Most Essential

E = Essential

LE = Least Essential

Table 4.11—Distribution of Chi-square values for value related competency group

Competency number	Teacher Educators					Primary Teachers					Teacher Trainees				
	ME	E	LE	CHI-Square Value	Level of Significance	ME	E	LE	CHI-Square Value	Level of Significance	ME	E	LE	CHI-Square Value	Level of Significance
3	82.5	17.5	0	113.5	0.01	77.5	22.5	0	95.5	0.01	79.5	20.5	0	102.3	0.01
6	77.5	22.5	0	95.5	0.01	76.0	23.5	0.5	89.9	0.01	81.5	18.5	0	109.6	0.01
8	57.0	33.0	10.0	33.2	0.01	66.5	29.5	4.0	59.3	0.01	36.0	57.5	6.5	39.4	0.01
36	20.5	64.5	15.0	44.2	0.01	33.5	58.0	8.5	36.7	0.01	14.0	50.0	36.0	19.8	0.01
44	54.5	43.0	2.5	44.8	0.01	53.0	45.0	2.0	45.2	0.01	57.5	40.0	2.5	47.4	0.01
45	18.0	64.5	17.5	43.7	0.01	34.5	59.0	6.5	41.4	0.01	14.0	41.0	45.0	17.1	0.01
48	26.0	58.0	16.0	28.9	0.01	21.5	69.5	9.0	61.2	0.01	11.0	81.5	7.5	104.7	0.01

for df(2) Chi-square value at 0.01 level is 9.210 and at 0.05 level it is 5.991

ME = Most Essential

E = Essential

LE = Least Essential

Table 4.12—Distribution of chi-square values for community related competency group

Competency number	Teacher Educators					Primary Teachers					Teacher Trainees				
	ME	E	LE	CHI-Square Value	Level of Significance	ME	E	LE	CHI-Square Value	Level of Significance	ME	E	LE	CHI-Square Value	Level of Significance
4	34.5	59.0	0	41.4	0.01	48.0	49.0	3.0	41.5	0.01	41.0	46.5	12.5	20.0	0.01
5*	19.0	59.0	0	29.8	0.01	32.0	58.0	10.0	34.6	0.01	28.0	33.5	38.5	1.6	N.S.
21	21.5	55.0	10.0	21.2	0.01	44.0	47.5	8.5	27.9	0.01	18.5	61.0	20.5	34.5	0.01
31	42.0	50.5	15.0	31.1	0.01	40.0	57.0	3.0	45.7	0.01	24.0	51.0	25.0	14.1	0.01

for df(2) Chi-square value at 0.01 level is 9.210 and at 0.05 level is 5.991

N.S = Non Significant

ME = Most Essential

E = Essential

LE = Least Essential

*denotes the competency is discarded

Table 4.13.—Distribution of chi-square values for pupil related competency group

Compe-tency number	Teacher Educators					Primary Teachers					Teacher Trainees				
	ME	E	LE	CHI-Square Value	Level of Signi-ficance	ME	E	LE	CHI-Square Value	Level of Signi-ficance	ME	E	LE	CHI-Square Value	Level of Signi-ficance
1	65.5	34.5	0	64.5	0.01	71.5	28.0	0.5	76.9	0.01	56.5	43.5	0	52.6	0.01
11	30.5	59.0	10.5	35.6	0.01	31.0	61.5	7.5	44.0	0.01	43.5	55.5	1.0	49.3	0.01
13	48.0	45.0	7.0	31.4	0.01	55.0	40.5	4.5	27.1	0.01	56.5	41.0	2.5	35.6	0.01
14	31.0	56.0	13.0	28.0	0.01	35.5	59.0	5.5	43.2	0.01	48.0	52.0	0	57.0	0.01
17	45.0	35.5	19.5	4.97	N.S	36.0	55.0	9.0	32.1	0.01	48.0	46.5	5.5	34.9	0.01
20	30.0	55.0	15.0	24.5	0.01	41.0	51.0	8.0	30.4	0.01	31.5	61.0	7.5	43.1	0.01
26*	32.0	41.0	27.0	3.02	N.S	24.5	60.0	15.5	33.2	0.01	31.0	55.0	14.0	25.4	0.01
27	54.0	43.0	3.0	36.5	0.01	58.5	38.0	3.5	46.4	0.01	57.5	40.0	2.5	47.4	0.01
30	30.0	63.5	6.5	49.3	0.01	38.0	53.0	9.0	30.1	0.01	17.5	65.0	17.5	45.1	0.01
34	57.0	33.0	10.0	33.2	0.01	57.0	35.5	7.5	37.0	0.01	67.5	31.5	1.0	66.3	0.01
35	43.0	53.0	4.0	40.3	0.01	46.0	47.0	5.0	36.1	0.01	21.5	53.5	25.0	18.6	0.01

(Contd...)

1	2	3	4	5	6	7	8	9	10	11	12	13	14	15	16
39	30.5	64.5	5.5	52.8	0.01	49.0	47.5	3.5	40.1	0.01	46.0	54.0	0	51.0	0.01
46	28.0	64.0	8.0	48.4	0.01	49.0	47.5	3.5	40.1	0.01	46.0	54.0	0	51.0	0.01
46	28.0	64.0	8.0	48.4	0.01	39.0	57.0	4.0	43.6	0.01	27.0	66.5	6.5	56.0	0.01
47	30.0	57.0	13.0	44.7	0.01	32.0	62.0	6.0	47.2	0.01	16.5	30.5	53.0	20.4	0.01

for df(2) Chi-square value at 0.01 level is 9.210 and at 0.05 level it is 5.991

ME = Most Essential

E = Essential

LE = Least Essential

*denotes that the competency is discarded for consideration

Table 4.14—Distribution of chi-square values for curriculum related competency group

Competency number	Teacher Educators					Primary Teachers					Teacher Trainees				
	ME	E	LE	CHI-Square Value	Level of Significance	ME	E	LE	CHI-Square Value	Level of Significance	ME	E	LE	CHI-Square Value	Level of Significance
15	64.5	34.5	1.0	60.6	0.01	57.5	41.0	1.5	49.7	0.01	65.0	35.0	0	63.5	0.01
16	40.0	48.5	11.5	22.5	0.01	43.0	53.5	3.5	41.7	0.01	31.5	60.0	8.5	39.9	0.01
18	69.0	30.0	1.0	69.9	0.01	63.0	33.0	4.0	52.3	0.01	64.0	35.0	1.0	59.7	0.01
41	17.0	70.0	13.0	60.8	0.01	36.0	54.5	9.5	30.7	0.01	25.0	66.5	8.5	52.2	0.01

for df (2) Chi-square value at 0.01 level is 9.210 and at 0.05 level it is 5.991.

ME = Most Essential

E = Essential

LE = Least Essential

DATA ANALYSIS FOR FINDING OUT THE "MOST ESSENTIAL" COMPETENCIES

Most essential competencies are the ones without which a teacher cannot become a competent person. These are highly required skills for a person entering teaching profession at primary level.

After dividing the competencies into various groups, performing Chi-square test and eliminating from the list the competencies which are not significant, the most essential characteristics from each group have been found out and then the complete list of most essential characteristics is taken from all the groups. The method of finding out the most essential competencies is given in the following pages.

To find out the most essential characteristics from the six groups, the highest percentage of preference given by teacher educator, primary teachers and teacher trainees under the option 'most essential' has been taken up. To know exactly their preference, a cut off score of 50 per cent has been taken as a minimum percentage in each category i.e., teacher educator, primary teachers and teacher trainees, under the option "Most Essential". This information gives the Most Essential competencies desired commonly by all the three types of respondents. Thus, the most essential characteristics have been found out from the six groups under the option most essential preferred by all the three types of respondents—teacher educators, primary teachers and teacher trainees.

Managerial related competencies

Competencies nos. 2,9,23,24,37,38,42 in the table 4.2 preferred by all the three types of respondents teacher educators, primary teachers and teacher trainees commonly. Table no. 4.9 shows that in each competency the preference is either 50 per cent or more than 50 per cent in the above cases under 'Most Essential' alternative. Hence, the four competencies under managerial related competencies are given below with competency numbers in brackets from table no.4.2.

1. The teacher should realise the significance and relevance of teaching. (Competency no.2)
2. The teacher should be everready to learn new things and constantly augment his knowledge base. (Competency no.9)
3. The teacher should motivate pupils and incite interest in them to learn. (Competency no.23)
4. The teacher should maintain discipline in classroom to facilitate smooth instruction. (Competency no.24)
5. The teacher should be a resourceful person. (Competency no. 37)
6. The teacher should be hard working. (Competency no. 38)
7. The teacher should develop easy, original and innovative methods to aid instruction. (Competency no.42)

Similarly the same criteria explained above is applied to the following competencies also and the results are as under.

School Related Competencies

It has been found that no competency is preferred by the three types of respondents under most essential category.

Community Related Competencies

It has been found that no competency is preferred by the three types of respondents under 'most essential' category when the above method is applied.

Value Related Competencies

Competencies which are preferred 'most essential' are nos. 3,6 and 44 in table no. 4.4.

1. The teachers should be honest and sincere. (Competency no. 3).
2. The teacher should love his profession. (Competency no. 6).

3. The teacher should develop moral values in children by giving striking examples from real life situations. (Competency no.44)

Pupil Related Competencies

The competencies preferred as most essential are competencies no's. 1,27,34 in table no. 4.5. They are as follows.

1. The teacher should be in intimate contact with students and be friendly with them. (Competency no.1)
2. The teacher should stimulate, impress and inspire students not only by his teaching but by his personality also. (Competency no. 27)
3. The teacher should identify the latent talents and aptitudes in students and try to draw out the best in them. (Competency no. 34)

Curriculum Related Competencies

The 'most essential' competencies are competencies no's. 15 and 18 in table no. 4.7. in this chapter.

1. The teacher should know the aim goal and objectives of teaching the subject. (Competency no.15)
2. The teacher should plan his lesson well and know the skills of instructional management. (Competency no.18)

To summarise, the total number of competencies opted as 'most essential' by teacher educators, primary teachers and teacher trainees are fifteen. Of these, 15 competencies, 7 competencies are from 'managerial related competencies' group, 3 from value related competencies' group, 3 from 'pupil related competencies' group and 2 from 'curriculum related competencies' group. There is no representation of 'most essential competencies' from two groups— 'school related competencies' and 'community related competencies'.

Thus the 15 competencies which are preferred by all the three types of respondents, viz., teacher educators, primary teachers and teacher trainees are as follows.

1. The teacher should realise the relevance and significance of teaching.
2. The teacher should be everready to learn new things and constantly augment his knowledge base.
3. The teacher should motivate pupils and incite interest in them to learn.
4. The teacher should maintain discipline in classroom to facilitate smooth instruction.
5. The teacher should be a resourceful person.
6. The teacher should be hard working.
7. The teacher should develop easy, original and innovative methods to aid instruction.
8. The teacher should be honest and sincere.
9. The teacher should love his profession.
10. The teacher should develop moral values in children by giving striking examples from real life situations.
11. The teacher should be in intimate contact with students and be friendly with them.
12. The teacher should stimulate, impress, and inspire students not only by his teaching but his personality also.
13. The teacher should identify the latent talents in students and try to draw out the best in them.
14. The teacher should know the aims, goal and objectives of teaching the subject.
15. The teacher should plan his lesson well and know the skills of instructional management.

Thus, the 15 most essential competencies from the view point of 'teacher educators', primary teachers and teacher trainees have been found out.

Similarly "Essential competencies" are also found out by the researchers and the procedure adopted for finding them is discussed in the following pages.

DATA ANALYSIS FOR FINDING OUT ESSENTIAL COMPETENCIES

To find out essential competencies, the method of selection has been the same as it was in the case of finding out the most essential competencies.

A cut off score of 50 per cent is taken from the option 'essential' preferred by teacher educators, primary teachers and teacher trainees who gave preference to the alternative 'essential' for each competency. So, the competencies with either 50 per cent preference or above in 'essential' alternative preferred by all the three types of respondents is taken to find out the essential characteristics.

The manner by which the essential characteristics were identified from the statistical treatment explained above is detailed in the following pages for all the six groups.

Managerial related competencies

Managerial related competencies preferred as essential characteristics by teacher educators, primary teachers and teacher trainees are competencies nos. 19,25,40 (three) in table no. 4.2. They are:

1. The teacher should evaluate students performance from time to time and give appropriate work for the gifted and remedial work for the substandard. (Competency no.19).
2. The teacher should attend to various teacher training programmes and improve his teaching competency. (Competency no. 25).
3. The teacher should be cheerful and active. (Competency no. 40)

School related competencies

Under school related competencies only one competency no.43 is preferred as 'essential' in table no.4.3.

1. The teacher should communicate pupils progress in various areas-cognitive, affective and psychomotor to parents by conducting meetings with them regularly.

Value related competencies

The competencies opted by the respondents in this group are competencies no's 36 and 48, in table no. 4.4. They are:

1. The teacher should be aware of our cultural heritage and pass it on to students. (Competency no. 36).
2. The teacher must have consistent pattern in action and policy. (Competency no. 48).

Community related competencies

The competency opted by the respondents under this group is competency no. 31 in table no. 4.6.

1. The teacher must seek co-operation from the society and self-government institutions and ensure their participation to improve the quality of Primary education.

Pupil related competencies

The competencies opted by respondents under this group are competencies no's. 14,20,30 and 46 in table no. 4.5.

1. The teacher should keep in view the individual differences of intellect in students and adapt suitable teaching techniques. (Competency no. 14)
2. The teacher should encourage activity based learning among students (Competency no.20)
3. The teacher should posses guidance and counselling skills to organise guidance and counselling sessions for the needy and the maladjusted students (Competency no.30)
4. The teacher must be sympathetic and understanding in finding a solution to pupils' personal and academic problems. (Competency no. 46)

Curriculum related competencies

Under this group the competency opted as essential by teacher educators, primary teachers, teacher trainees is competency no. 41 in table no. 4.7.

1. The teacher should effectively relate the subject matter in one area to other areas of the curriculum. (Competency no. 41).

To summarise, competencies nos. 19,25 and 40 (three only) are taken from managerial competencies, competency no. 43 from school related competencies (one) competencies 36 and 48 (two only) from value related competencies, competency no. 31 from 'community related competencies' (one only) competencies no's 14,20,30 and 46 (four only) from the pupil related competencies, and competency no. 41 (one only) from curriculum related competency.

Thus a total number of 12 essential competencies have been identified and they are listed as follows:

1. The teacher should evaluate students' performance from time to time and give appropriate work for the gifted and remedial work for the substandard.
2. The teacher should attend to various teacher training programmes and improve his/her teaching competencies.
3. The teacher should be cheerful and active.
4. The teacher should communicate the pupils' progress in various areas—cognitive, affective and psychomotor to parents by conducting meetings with them regularly.
5. The teacher should be aware of our cultural heritage and pass it on to students.
6. The teacher must have consistent pattern in action and policy.
7. The teacher must seek co-operation from the society and self-government institutions and ensure their participation to improve the quality of education.

8. The teacher should keep in view the individual differences of intellect in students and adopt suitable teaching techniques.

9. The teacher should encourage activity based learning among students.

10. The teacher should posses guidance and counselling skills to organise guidance and counselling sessions for the needy and maladjusted students.

11. The teacher must be sympathetic and understanding in finding a solution to pupils' personal and academic problems.

12. The teacher should effectively relate the subject matter in one area to other areas of the curriculum.

Thus a total number of 27 necessary competencies are identified from six competency groups as viewed commonly by teacher educators, primary teachers and teacher trainees which are considered necessary for primary teachers. These necessary competencies include 15 "most essential" competencies without which an individual is considered **incompetent** to become a teacher. Further, even the 12 'Essential' competencies which are considered to be desirable for a teacher to better his/her teaching performance are included. So, out of 27 necessary competencies, 15 most essential competencies which are considered as **'most required'** for the teachers are identified by the researchers, Without the presence of these **'most essential'** competencies, the teacher is incompetent and it is better for the individual to change the profession or such individuals shouldn't be selected by the interviewing board during the recruitment of teachers.

The **12 essential competencies** are also found out which are to be considered as **desirable competencies** that should be present in teachers entering teaching profession. These competencies help the teachers to become better in the profession.

Thus the **necessary competencies** are found out by the researchers from the view point of teacher educators, primary teachers and teacher trainees including 15 most essential and 12 essential competencies.

Hence the Hypothesis no: 1 formulated as "A few competencies are necessary to be possessed by teachers as viewed commonly by teacher educators, primary teachers and also by the teacher trainees" is proved to be tenable and hence retained. Thus the first objective "To identify the necessary competencies to be possessed by teachers in general at primary level of education has been realised".

Similarly as discussed earlier in this chapter, fifteen "most essential" competencies are found out and the list of most essential competencies are given in page no. 97.

Hence the Hypothesis no:2 formulated as "Some most essential competencies do exist i teachers which are to be considered as an essential requirement for teachers entering teaching profession at primary level of education" is proved to be tenable and hence retained.

TECHNIQUES ADMINISTERED BY THE RESEARCHERS TO EMPOWER THE MOST ESSENTIAL COMPETENCIES IN TEACHERS

To find out the most essential competencies which a prospective teacher has to possess will not be sufficient, but it is necessary that some techniques have to be developed for empowering and nurturing the competencies in teachers so that they will become more competent to perform their duties efficiently in their profession. So, the researchers have suggested some techniques through which the teachers can be empowered with most essential competencies. The manner by which the techniques were suggested for empowerment of the teachers and the means and ways of empowerment are detailed in the following pages.

The researchers have administered the following techniques to empower the competencies in teachers. The detailed information of the techniques and how they can be helpful in empowerment of teachers is given in the following pages. The six techniques administered by the researchers for the teachers for empowerment are as follows.

1. Role-play
2. Modeling
3. Observation
4. Micro teaching
5. Seminar, Discussion, Symposium
6. Brain Storing

Role-play

Role-play is an informal and non-theatrical enactment of situation in which a trainee apply cognitive skills or experiments with behaviours in line with their training objectives. It relates to real organisational problems and the trainees involve themselves by performing different roles (during training in the class room), So, it is very interesting and highly enjoyable.

It is of two types, spontaneous and structured. A spontaneous role-play denotes that enactments in which a trainee describes an interaction between himself and other members. The trainer simply provides an issue of learning in line with the training objective and the trainee is asked to enact spontaneously.

The trainer provides feed-back on the role played and the scene is re-enacted. In a structured role-play, the trainer sets up a situation and illustrates a particular event to the learners. Each trainee, therefore, is given a hand out describing his roles called 'role belief'. At the end of the role play, feed back is taken from the trainee as well as it is given by the trainer on their role performance which provides reinforcement to their learning.

Teachers in 1950, began to study more closely about group techniques in their teaching. The work of Moren, Lewin and other field theorists prompted an interest in the pupils social environment, school climate, the influence of peer group and teaching of small group discussions. As a consequence teaching of role-play to improve group performance, thus raising the productiveness, became part of the training of many teachers. It was an aspect of teaching that had been experimented with and highly valued in the Soviet Union and had strongest emphasis during the cultural revolution of China in 1960s and 1970s.

Makerenko (1951) was an experimental teacher who placed emphasis on role-play in teaching. He experimentally proved that role play can develop features like teacher' style, pupil-teacher relationships, sense of productivity and collectivity in teachers. Style and tone, he wrote, 'have always been ignored in 'pedagogical theory' but, they were of greatest importance. Style can develop a sense of responsibility, and through style suitable and recognisable habits of behaviour can be developed and which in turn can create an inner and outward feelings of behaviours in pupils. The teacher's relationship with students is of great importance and Makerenko oriented his teaching sensitivity to pupils' interests, development of personality and future possibilities and created a lot of trust in them.

Modeling

It is evident from informal observation that human behaviour is transmitted, whether deliberately or inadvertently, largely through exposure to social models. Indeed it is true that Reichard (1938) noted many years ago, in many languages "The word for 'teach' is the same as the word for 'show'. It is difficult to imagine a culture in which language, mores, vocational activities, familiar customs, and educational religious and political practices, are gradually shaped in each new member by direct consequences of their trial and error performances without benefit of models. In many instances people pattern their behaviour after models. It is also possible to regulate human behaviour through modeling and research. Social learning theory by A. Bandura greatly emphasises this aspect. Modeling process is highly valued since the tremendous research performed by Bandura and as a consequence 'modeling' became an indispensable technique to develop attitudes, complexes, occupational and social competencies in individuals.

There are many reasons why modeling influences are heavily favoured in promoting everyday learning. Bandura's (1971) own observations on modeling influence is as follows: "In laboratory investigations experimenters arrange comparatively begin environments in which errors donot create fatal consequences for the organism. By contrast, natural environments are loaded with potentially lethal consequences for those unfortunate enough to perform hazardous errors. For this reason it is exceedingly injudicious to rely on differential reinforcement of trial-and-error performances in teaching children to learn, adolescents to drive automobiles and medical students to perform surgeries, and adult to develop complex social and occupational competencies. Had experimental situations been made more realistic so that animals toiling in skinner boxes were drowned, electrocuted and dismembered, or extensively bruised for the errors that invariably occur during early phases of unguided learning, the limitations of instrumental conditioning would have been forcefully revealed".

The other psychologists also have a favourable opinion on modeling influences and the following observations made by them emphasise the fact.

Where desired forms of behaviour can be conveyed only by social cues, modeling is an indispensable aspect of learning. Even in instances where it is possible to establish new responses patterns through other means acquisition can be considerably shortened by providing appropriate models. (Bandura and Mc.Donald 1963; Luchins and Luchins, 1966. John Chesler Bartlett and Victor, 1968).

A great deal of research has been published on the 'types of people who are most responsive to modeling influences, and the kinds of models most likely to evoke imitative behaviour from others'. (Bandura and Watters, 1963; Campbell, 1961; Flanders, 1968).

It is often reported that persons who lack self esteem, feel incompetent, or who have been frequently rewarded for imitative responses, are especially prone to adopt the behaviour of successful models.

It has been abundantly documented in social-psychological research (Bandura, 1969; Blake, 1958; Campbell, 1961) that models who are high in prestige, power, intelligence and competence are emulated to a considerably greater degree than models of sub-ordinate standing.

Models charateristics exert the greatest influence on imitation under conditions in which individuals can observe the models behaviour but not its consequences when the value of modeled behaviour is not revealed, observers must rely on such cues as clothing, linguistic style, general appearance, age, sex, likeableness, and various competencies and social symbols as the basis for judging the probable efficiency of the modeled models of response.

In Bandura's (1969) theory of social learning conceptualisation, learning by observation is said to occur principally through the informative function of modeling influences, and is governed by competent process; attending, retention, motor reproduction and motivation.

According to Bandura, attending refers to the observer's selective perception of the significant features of the model, while retention refers to the maintenance in permanent memory of a symbolic form of patterns which have been attended to in the model. It is an advanced capacity for symbolic representation which enables human to learn much of their behaviour by observation with the symbolic codes allowing for the retention of large quantities of information in easily stored form. Motor reproduction refers to translation of symbolic representations into actions on their use as guides for actions, while motivation refers tot he rewardingness of enacting the modelled behaviours. Thus in Bandura' model the process of attending and retention refer to acquisition of behaviour or skills, motor reproduction refers to performance, while motivation to acquisition and performance.

Observation

Two images of the teacher performance recur in literature—that of the 'expressive artist' whose unique style is a subtle blend of personality and acquired technique; and that of the 'master craftsman' who developed a repertoire of the skills of his trade. The artist image is inseparable from the growth paradigm and its emphasis on personality and style suggests autonomy and quality but not flexibility. Craftsman however can acquire new skills through constant observation of the 'master craftsman' at work, eventhough the process is likely to be lengthy; but the process more likely to be permanant also (Joyce, 1980).

Performance is improved by more and more observation, discussion and experimenting with only an occasional need for guided practice in any specified skill or competency.

Most performing occupations offer considerable opportunity to 'observe' master performers at work, both before and after initial training. The promising musician for example not only strives to hear and see famous players but deliberately arranges to study with more than one teacher for substantial periods, and to take master classes for others. Similarly in practitioners in surgery also learning to handle difficult cases is attained by observing several experts and having them explain their strategies and thoughts. It is this training type of observation which makes them competent in teaching profession and distinguishes professional trainers from apprenticeship, but teachers are generally not offered such an opportunity. By constant observation, competencies and value like dedication, responsibility interest can be empowered along with the quality in their teaching profession.

Micro-teaching

It was Keith Acheson, a research scholar in the Stanford University who discovered that video-type recorder could be used to provide feed back of demonstration lesson. He along with other students of the Stanford University started using video tape recorder for modifying the behaviour of teacher trainees. After some time it was Dwight Allen of Standord University who coined the term 'micro-teaching'. Later, many other in U.S.A., U.K. and Netherlands did pioneering work in micro-teaching. Micro-teaching was introduced in India in 1967.

It is planned to develop new teaching skills and analyse the existing ones. The technique provides teaching practice in a situation in which the complexities of the class room are minimized by restricting the number of pupils and length of the lesson and by focusing on specific teaching skills. Micro-teaching programmes last from 5 to 20 minutes, are based on teaching skills, for e.g., closing a lesson or gaining participation, and use various audio-visual aids in demonstration of micro-teaching principles. A global teaching practice may end a micro-teaching course in order to integrate the individual skills in teaching, or micro-teaching sessions may be more discrete in nature. Micro-teaching may be used to produce models of teaching or to illustrate the group dynamics of the class room.

Micro-teaching provides an opportunity for teacher trainee or experienced teacher to acquire new teaching skills and to refine old ones. It involves the following stages.

— the analysis of teaching skills in behavioural terms.

— demonstration of teaching skills on video tapes or in class room .

— the trainee plans a short lesson in the subject of his interest in which he can use his teaching skill.

— feed back is provided to the student-teachers who observe and analyse his lesson with the help of a supervisor.

— the feed back and supervisor's remarks provide an insight to the student teacher in the use of teaching skill. He plans the lesson in order to use the skill more efficiently second time.

For effective result, some background materials, areas of discussion, and areas of expected solutions should be drafted in advance which should be used as basic inputs for the workshop.

Discussion

The discussion method of teaching is a process in which a small group assembles to communicate with each other—using speaking, listening and non-verbal processes.

Oliver and Shaver (1966) developed a jurisprudential model of instruction, which makes use of discussion to achieve the learning outcome. Hill (1977) and many other educators advocated the use of discussion (supplemented by text book study) for promoting critical thinking and other cognitive objectives. Discussion paves the way for review of key concepts in a subject, integration of subject matter with other knowledge, application of subject matter and evaluation of subject taught. Discussion also helps to develop attitudes and values. Early philosophers and educationists like Socrates, Plato, Aristotle, Descartes used this discussion method to advance their pupil's capability for moral reasoning.

Seminar

A seminar is a small group of persons meeting to discuss or study a particular topic with a teacher. Seminar is generally used to refer to a structural group discussion, that may precede or follow a formal lecture, often in the form of an essay or a paper presentation. The audience critically evaluate the paper and discuss the facts or findings of the paper (Sah, A.K. 1991).

The major advantages of the seminar is its stimulation and testing of the participants' power of comprehension and evaluation. The presenter is tested on his skill in arranging and formulating a sustained agreement.

Symposium

It is a small conference for discussion of a particular subject. Symposium is a discussion by different specialists or speakers on the same topic, emphasizing or dealing with different aspects of the same topic. The audience seldom participate, as the chairperson and speakers anticipate possible questions and doubts to be cleared and incorporated in their presentations. It is in this aspect that a symposium differs mainly from a panel discussion or a seminar. The symposium gives full details of the topic to the audience. The speakers get trained in self-study, and expression of thought.

Brain Storming

Oxford Advanced Learner's Dictionary defines Brainstorming as a method of solving problems in which all the members of a group suggest ideas which are then discussed.

It is an unstructured form of learning first developed by Alex Osborn in 1938. Under this technique, the trainees form a group like a conference and a problem is passed to them. The trainees attempt to find a solution by generating and amassing all the ideas they can, irrespective of strange, unusual, outrageous, practical or impracticable suggestions, on the problems without any analysis or evaluation. At a later stage, all the ideas or suggestions, are analysed, synchronised and evaluated to get unique and practical solution which is also done by the group.

This technique generates creative thinking, highly participative discussions and produce good results. This is effective for problem solving, creating team spirit, getting qualitative solutions of the problem.

ESTABLISHING VALIDITY OF THE PROCESSES

This initiation training for empowering teachers is being taken up as an experimental aspect. It is preferred to focus only on a small sample of 15 teachers as was suggested by a team of experts who were contacted for the purpose.

So, as suggested by the experts, the researchers have taken a sample of 15 in-service teachers who were pursuing their B.Ed. course through in-service programme in three Colleges of Education in Krishna District, Andhra Pradesh. Five teachers from each college were taken up. The teachers were having a minimum of 3 years of teaching experience and were working in Mandal Parishad Primary schools as Secondary Grade Assistants teaching at primary level for classes I to V.

Teachers with different methodologies like Mathematics, English, Physical Sciences and Social Studies were taken up. All the teachers possessed Teacher Training Certificate from DIETs besides a certificate in graduation.

Before administering the techniques to teachers, the researchers have explained clearly the objectives of the study to the teachers. The researchers requested them to extend their co-operation for the study and then taken the consent of teachers to carry out the study on them.

The researchers have taken the permission of the principals of the three training colleges to carry out the study on teachers. The researchers requested the teachers to permit him to observe them while they take classes regularly during their in-service training programme. Thus the 15 teachers were observed for a period of one month. The researchers have observed three classes for every teacher and for all the 15 teachers the researcher had made classroom observations, and noted the pre-test scores basing on the observations made in the classrooms. The mode of scoring, and method of observation made by the researchers are given in the following paragraphs.

Scoring procedure and Class room observations of the teachers before the administration of the techniques

Observation and method of scoring are done in the following manner. For every teacher, three classes were observed as per the advice given by the experts. The researchers made the observations of teachers by observing the behaviours expressed by them for every competency during their period of classroom instruction.

The competencies (most essential) and the corresponding behaviours to be observed under the respective competency are noted down by the researchers. The researchers noted down the scores obtained by the teacher during the classroom instruction by observing the behaviours expressed by the teacher in the class room. The researchers observed three classes for every teacher and for 15 competency statements, 30 behaviours were observed. The researchers found out if the particular behaviour is expressed by the teacher under the particular competency. The main purpose of taking behaviours into account and finding out if they are expressed or not in the classroom by the teacher is that,

a) behaviours can be measured quantitatively and depending upon the intensity with which the behaviour is expressed scoring can be done relatively in an easier way when compared to measuring competencies directly without a system of quantitative measurement.

b) value related competencies like "the teacher should love his/her profession", "the teacher should be honest and sincere", are very difficult to measure as they are highly abstract and qualitative. So some kind of quantitative measures should be taken to measure these competencies. Similarly competencies like the "teacher should be hardworking", "teacher should be resourceful", "teacher should realize the significance and relevance of teaching", competencies under managerial related group, should also have a proper method of measurement and scoring. Hence the researchers have found out 30 behaviours for 15 competencies to make the scoring procedure quantitative. The scoring procedure adopted by the researchers is as follows:

During the classroom observations made by the researchers before administering the techniques for empowerment in teachers the following scoring procedure had been followed. For every teacher a maximum of three classes were observed by the researchers. A score of 0 was awarded if the behaviour was not expressed by the teacher in the even once in the class. Similarly, a score of '1'was awarded if each behaviour was expressed one time in the class. In the same way a score of '2' was given if the teacher had expressed each behaviour two times in the class room and a score of '3' was awarded if the teacher had expressed that particular behaviour under the respective competency for three times.

The researchers, in order to get more reliable information regarding the teaching procedure in the class room, the motivational aspect of the pupils in the form of questions put by them to the teacher was also taken before and after the administration of techniques along with the behaviours the teachers expressed in the class room. If every student asks at least one question pertaining to the subject in the class room while the teacher engages the class, (with the strength of the class at a maximum of 40 students), it was considered to be a highly motivated class by the researchers and a score of 3.0 was awarded to the teacher. Similarly, if 10 per cent to 50 per cent of students ask questions pertaining to the subject, a score of 2.0 was awarded to the teacher.

In the same way if 10 per cent of students had asked the questions pertaining to subject a score of 1.0 was given to the teacher and if no student asked the questions a score of 0 was given to the teacher.

So basing on the intensity of behaviours expressed by the teacher in the class room by observing the classes and scoring procedure adopted as explained above the researchers have categorised the scoring in the following manner.

Scores		Category of behaviour Present in Teacher
0	-	Not existing
1	-	Trace
2	-	Satisfactory
3	-	Sufficient

A score of 0 denotes that the behaviour is not expressed by the teacher even once in the class room and accordingly the behaviour was categorised as "not existing". If the behaviour is expressed one time by the teacher, it was categorised as "trace". Similarly, if the behaviour is expressed 2 times in the class, it was categorised as "satisfactory" and in the same way if it is expressed 3 or more times the behaviour was categorised as "sufficiently" present in the teacher at the time of engaging the class.

For every teacher, the researchers have noted down the behaviours of only those teachers whose scores were either 0 or 1, i.e., if the particular behaviour is either "not existing" or present in a "trace" respectively. The remaining expressed behaviours whose scores were 2 or 3 (satisfactory or sufficient) for teachers were not taken into consideration for the reason that those behaviours were already pre-existing in them to "satisfactory and sufficient" degree respectively. The researchers have used Teacher No. 1, Teacher No.2, etc., instead of using their names to keep their names confidentially. Thus the pre-test scores for 15 teachers were taken by the researcher after carefully making the observations in the classroom. The details of pre-test and post-test scores in order to make comparision of the fifteen teachers easily the researchers have put the pre-test and post-test scores in the same table separately for the fifteen teachers. The details are given the following pages.

The details of the 15 most essential competency statements, the bahaviours observed under each competency, the techniques administered are given in the following table no. 4.15.

Table 4.15—Most essential competencies, behaviurs observed by the researchers for the teachers and techniques administered for empowerment

Name of the Group	Competency Statement	Behaviours observed under each competency	Techniques Administered for empowerment
1. MANAGERIAL RELATED COMPETENCIES	1. The teacher should be ever ready to learn new things and constantly augment his/her knowledge base.	a) The teacher regularly reads book pertaining to the subject, discusses important concepts with subject experts and seniors to increase his/her knowledge base.	Seminar and Discussion
		b) The teacher expresses willingness to attend workshop, inservice training programmes to know the latest techniques of teaching.	
	2. The teacher should realise the relevance and significance of teaching.	a) The teacher utilises all the available opportunities that are beneficial to the students viz., field trips, science fares, sports and games.	
		b) The teacher teaches all the units of syllabus without fail, if necessary, by taking some special classes.	Seminar and Discussion

(Contd...)

1	2	3	4
	3. the teacher should motivate pupils and incite interest in them to learn.	a) The teacher keeps on changing for novel and play way methods to teach new concepts.	
		b) The teacher tries to learn and prepare different types of charts and models to teach in the class, encourages them to succeed in various planned activities by assisting them.	Role-play and Observation
	4. The teacher should maintain discipline in classroom to facilitate smooth instruction.	a) The teacher identifies with the class and never allows monotony to set in by quick shift of presentation.	Role-play and Observation
		b) the teacher interacts freely with students and at the same time avoids giving excessive freedom by arresting deviated or irrelevant talks and questions of the students.	
	5. The teacher should be a resourceful person.	a) Clarifies all the doubts of the students convincingly resulting in students' happiness.	Discussion and Symposium
		b) Voluntarily approaches the pupils to know their problems and tries to solve them convincingly.	

	6. The teacher should be hard working.	a) The teacher corrects the homework of the students by pin-pointing their mistakes. b) The teacher collects more information and material to make the lesson interesting and absorbing.	Seminar and Discussion
	7. The teacher should develop easy, original and innovative methods to aid instruction.	a) The teacher develops low-cost aids by using the material available in school. b) The teacher involves pupils in preparing teaching aids like charts, models to explain concepts relating to mathematics sciences, languages and arts.	Brain storming Modeling and Observation
2. VALUE RELATED COMPETENCIES	8. The teacher should be honest and sincere.	a) The teacher discharges his/her duties with time sense like attending to school regularly, taking classes regularly and working for the academic and personality development of the pupils. b) The teacher attends to school work entrusted, by developing his/her our resources and does it by using best capabilities.	Observation Role-play

(Contd...)

1	2	3	4
	9. The teacher should love his/her profession.	a) The teacher works and teaches for extra time for the benefit of children even when the payment of remuneration for the extra time does not exist.	Role-play
		b) The teacher attends to his school work on priority and then executes other responsibilities like family rituals, social functions etc.	
	10. The teacher should develop moral values in children by giving striking examples from real life situations.	a) The teacher uses simulated situations and reinforces the experted behaviour when exhibited.	Role-play
		b) The teacher organises small role-plays and drama and makes the children get the feeling of the 'roles' they enact.	and Observation
3. PUPIL RELATED COMPETENCIES	11. The teacher should be in intimate contact with students and be friendly with them.	a) The teacher creates a feeling of love and concern for them by attending individually to their academic and personal problems.	
		b) The teacher doesn't snub or hurt the students by showing their defects; instead, encourages, helps and shows them the way in which they can overcome their lapses.	Role-play and Observation.

	12. The teacher should stimulate, impress and inspire students not only by his teaching but by his/her personality also.	a) The teacher believes and behaves with pleasant manners, habits and approaches. b) The teacher promotes pupils' curiosity and interest by clarifying their doubts with appreciation and always speaks good encouraging language.	Modeling and Observation
	13. The teacher should identify the latent talents in students and try to draw out the best in them.	a) The teacher encourages pupils to participate in drawing and painting competitions, elocution, debate, essay writing, science fares etc. and gives them sufficient guidance. b) The teacher maintains an anecdotal record and explores opportunities for his pupils.	Micro-teaching Observation Discussion
4. CURRICULUM RELATED COMPETENCIES	14. The teacher should know the aim, goal and objectives of teaching the subject.	a) The teacher makes the children attain the optimum levels of teaching. b) The teacher engages students in activities like preparing the charts, clay models and other aids so that the three domains are achieved.	Seminar and Discussion
	15. The teacher should have lesson planning skill and instruction management.	a) The teacher plans the lesson with clarity including what to teach; time allotment for a period of 30 or 45 mts. b) The teacher plans with easy-moderate-difficult examples to meet the needs of all the students in the class.	Micro-teaching Modeling Observation Discussion

DETAILS OF COMPETENCY STATEMENTS, BEHAVIOURS OBSERVED FOR EVERY TEACHER UNDER EACH COMPETENCY

1. The teacher should be everready to learn new things and constantly augment his knowledge base (please refer to table no. 4.15).

Knowledge is an unending process and with the increase in exploration of knowledge, the teacher should also keep himself afloat with the ever increasing knowledge. For this, he has to read a good number of books pertaining to the subject besides attending to inservice training programmes and participating in seminars and workshops. An incompetent teacher who doesn't keep pace with the increasing knowledge can't fulfil the academic needs of his pupils.

Behaviours observed under this competency are

a. The teacher regularly reads books pertaining to the subject, discusses important concepts with subject experts and seniors to increase his/her knowledge base.

b. The teacher expresses willingness to attend workshop, inservice training programmes to know the latest techniques of teaching.

2. The teacher should realise the relevance and significance of teaching (please refer to table no. 4.15).

A significant teacher has a special or suggestive meaning in teaching. He should know the importance and purpose of teaching. Unless he possesses firm belief and faith in what he teaches, he can't teach it effectively. The language teacher should know the purpose of teaching a language and the benefits of teaching it. Similarly the Mathematics and Science teachers must know the utility and importance of teaching those subjects on a broader perspective. Those teachers should utilise every opportunity for making the relevance and significance of what they teach and also to make students realise the purpose of learning by making regular visits to near by factories in the name of field trips and participating in science fares, etc.

Behaviours observed under this competency

a. The teacher utilises all the available opportunities that are beneficial to the students viz., field trips, science fares, sports and games.

b. The teacher teaches all the units of syllabus without fail, if necessary, by taking some special classes.

3. The teacher should motivate pupils and incite interest in them to learn. (Please refer to table no. 4.15)

A good number of pyschologists, educationists have realised the importance of motivation in learning and the role of motivation in creating interest in pupils to learn. Only when a teacher is instrinscially motivated to perform his duties sincerely, he can create and sustain interest in pupils to learn. This competency has a great utility value especially for teachers who work in various schools in rural areas at primary level, where pupils attendance is generally low. Unless the teacher creates an interesting classroom environment and motivate pupils, the pupils may not turn up to school in good numbers and take interest in learning.

Behaviours observed under this competency are

a. The teacher keeps on changing for novel and play way methods to teach new concepts.

b. The teacher tries to learn and prepare different types of charts and models to teach in the class, encourages them to succeed in various planned activities by assisting them.

4. The teacher should maintain discipline in classroom to facilitate instruction smoothly (please refer to table no, 4.15).

Maintaining discipline in the classroom is one of the foremost requisites of teacher. Though a teacher is knowledgeable person, if he fails to control the indiscipline and other minor distractions in the class room, the purpose of instruction will be defeated. However it is better for the teacher to play the role of a facilitator rather than a rigid one in the class room and thus inculate self-discipline in students. Hence the teacher should first control the class room and see that pupils' attention is not diverted by outward distractions by shifting the presentation by changing voice and tone, by cutting a joke and thus avoid monotony in the class.

Behaviours observed under this competency are

a. The teacher identifies with the class and never allows monotony to set in by quick shift of presentation.

b. The teacher interacts freely with students and at the same time avoids giving excessive freedom by arresting deviated or irrelevant talks and questions of the students.

5. The teacher should be a resourceful person. (please refer to table no. 4.15.)

A resourceful teacher is good or quick at finding answers to questions and has many pertinent illustrations. A resourceful teacher posses the ability to deal promptly and effectively with problems and quick at finding solutions to problems. If a teacher is resourceful, he can become a reliable individual for the institution and can guide his students by giving a lot of information in the field of education. Especially, keeping in view the tremendous progress that has occurred in educational technologies and allied fields, a teacher should be resourceful and should be handy with the latest developments in education.

Behaviours observed under this competency are

a. The teacher clarifies all the doubts of the students convincingly resulting in students' happiness.

b. The teacher voluntarily approaches the pupils to know their problems and tries to solve them convincingly.

6. The teacher should be hard-working (please refer to table no. 4.15)

A hardworking teacher works with care and energy and believes that his/her own best work has resulted from long hardwork. He is painstaking and careful. A hardworking teacher gives additional information on the subject, is dedicated, engage in original and intelligent work and is painstaking. Hardworking and resourcefulness go hand in hand. Hardworking is the one of the most essential characteristics a teacher should possess. Without hardwork, a teacher can't be successful in his profession.

Behaviours observed under this competency are

a. The teacher corrects the homework of the students by pin-pointing their mistakes.

b. The teacher collects more information and material to make the lesson interesting and absorbing.

7. The teacher should develop easy, original and innovative methods to aid instruction. (please refer to table no. 4.15)

An innovative teacher uses what seems to be original and relatively unique devices to aid instruction. The teacher believes in originality in preference to good judgement. This is perfectly true especially to teachers dealing Science subjects which demand a lot of models and devices to facilitate better learning of concepts. Low cost aids, models prepared with clay etc., naturally incite interest in children and they leave an indelible impression on their minds and they can also facilitate better understanding of the concepts. Hence, the teacher should always engage his mind thinking about the appropriate and relevant methods which help the students in learning.

Behaviours observed under this competency are

a. The teacher develops low-cost aids by using the material available in school.

b. The teacher involves pupils in preparing teaching aids like charts, models to explain concepts relating to Mathematics, sciences, languages and arts.

8. The teacher should be honest and sincere. (please refer to table no. 4.15)

A sincere teacher doesnot pretend and accept pupil's efforts as sincere. Teacher shows what appeared to be sincere with a pupil' view point.

Honesty is the clear conscience "before myself and before my fellow humanbeings". Honesty is the awareness of what is right and appropriate in one's role, one's behaviour, and one's relationship. For eg., the teacher who exactly arrives in time to school and leaves the campus doesn't necessarily imply honesty on his part. The teacher should continuously apply the principles which work at best for his students, for himself and society and ethics and values which make classroom functional and useful. When there is say a word of praise from others this work as tremendous incentive and boosts· up his belief in honesty and sincerity. Honesty and sincerity generally go together and one cannot function effectively without the other.

Behaviours observed under this competency are

a. The teacher discharges his/her duties with time sense like attending to school regularly, taking classes regularly and working for the academic and personality development of the pupils.

b. The teacher attends to school work entrusted, by developing his/her own resources and does it by using best capabilities.

9. The teacher should love his profession. (please refer to table no. 4.15)

'Love' is not simply a desire, a passion, an intense feeling for one person or object, but a consciousness which is simultaneously selfless and self-fulfilling. For a teacher love towards his profession is developed when he knows by experience the nobility of a profession. Every individual first loves 'himself' or 'self' more than anything else. Just for a minute, if he substitutes himself in the place of a person in distress, then he can develop a pity in himself for others. From pity arises love. It is a concern for remaining optimistic and develop a positive attitude towards the profession. Love doesn't' mean dwelling on the weaknesses of others; instead a concern for removing one's own defects. The teacher should regularly monitor his own 'self' and adopt the natural habit of giving to his students by creating a love in them towards education and constantly check one's own 'pulse' since 'conscience' is the best judge. When one has a balance of love and power in words, this gives others compassion and love.

Behaviours observed under this competency are

a. The teacher works and teaches for extra time for the benefit of children even when the payment of remuneration for the extra time does not exist.

b. The teacher attends to school work on priority and then executes other responsibilities like family rituals, social functions etc.

10. The teacher should develop moral values in children by giving striking examples, from real life situations. (please refer to table no. 4.15)

'Morality' is the final out put of the qualities like being sincere, honest, love and responsibility. In a nut shell it is the 'Dharma' and selfless service sacrificing one's own 'ego and resisting others by not succumbing to heinous acts which hurt others. The person who observes morality conquers 'Aham' (ego) and at the same time renders his 'duty' by performing 'selfless' service. It is the highest phase of one's own life.

The teacher can inculcate the values such as kindness, sympathy and altruism by taking examples of persons who finally tasted defeat by being immoral in their lives. The permanence and relative advantages of being moral can be taught by giving standing examples of Alexander, Hitler, Mussolini, Napoleon on one hand and the examples of Lord Buddha, Lord Christ, Mother Teresa, Swami Vivekananda should be given so that children can realise the right path to be followed.

The teacher can praise time and again pupils who show honesty so that they donot stoop to undesirable means when they are under tremendous pressure from their surrounding environmental factors. They should be taught the later consequences of bad qualities though one enjoys its fruits momentarily.

Behaviours observed under this competency are

a. The teacher uses simulated situations and reinformces the experted behaviour when exhibited.

b. The teacher organises small role-plays and dramas and makes the children get the feeling of the 'roles' they enact.

11. The teacher should be in intimate contact with children and be friendly with them. (please refer to table no. 4.15)

Children, who enter pre-primary or primary school have a thousand questions in their minds. After spending a joyful life in homes, they feel reluctant to enter the school campus. The mechanistic school time-table the routine classes, the rigid home-work, all these perplex their little minds. To add this, the teacher appears as the person whom they fear most. Exactly at this critical hour, the role of a teacher becomes a great task. If the teacher creates a feeling of love and affection in their minds and removes their initial inhibitions and fear complexes, the young ones begin to develop a liking for school. A friendly gesture, spending some jolly time with children, teaching them through joyful methods etc activities from teacher remove the distance barrier and brings children in close contact with their teacher.

Behaviours observed under this competency are

a. The teacher creates a feeling of love and concern for them by attending individually to their academic and personal problems.

b. The teacher doesn't snub or hurt the students by showing their defects instead, encourages, helps and shows them the way in which they can overcome their lapses.

12. The teacher should stimulate, impress and inspire students not only by his teaching but by his personaltiy also. (please refer to table no. 4.15)

It is a matter of common sense that some individuals possess some qualities from which other persons take inspiration. Almost every successful individual draws inspiration one way or the other from his 'guru' or teacher. This holds good for any other profession or for that matter any field. The qualities like punctuality, promptness, leadership, character, judgement and reasoning, commitment, etc., combine to form the so called 'personality'. Especially if a teacher possesses these qualities and puts them in practice in his daily life, thousands of students draw inspiration from him and imbibe some of these qualities in them. Generally children are easily attracted towards the manners of their teachers and try to imitate them. Hence the teacher must inspire and impress students by standing himself as an example and try to inculcate virtues in children.

Behaviours observed under this competency are

a. The teacher believes and behaves with pleasant manners, habits and approaches

b. The teacher promotes pupils' curiosity and interest by clarifying their doubts with appreciation and always speaks good encouraging language.

13. The teacher should identify the latent talents in students and try to draw out the best in them. (please refer to table no. 4.15)

Every individual is possessed with some talent innately and the teacher should try to identify it. Some pupils possess a natural inclination towards subjects like Mathematics, Sciences and some towards humanities. Some have a liking for fine arts, music and dance. The teacher, if identifies the innate talents in students and provide proper training, these innate abilities can be developed. If a student has an inclination towards a particular subject and erroneously places himself in some other field he wastes his natural ability and cannot show progress in that area. Hence it is the duty of a teacher to identify this talent early and provide sufficient feed back and encouragement for the student. As a result, he can introduce artists, musicians, players and other persons to the world. Infact, great painters, great players and musicians take birth as a result of the identification of their talent by their 'Guru' at the right time.

Behaviours observed under this competency are

a. The teacher encourages pupils to participate in drawing and painting competitions, elocutions, debate, essay writing, science fares etc. and gives them sufficient guidance.

b. The teacher maintains an anecdotal record and explores opportunities for his/her pupils.

14. The teacher should know the aims, goals and objectives of teaching the subject. (please refer to table no. 4.15)

The teacher should have clear understanding regarding the goals, aims and objectives of the subject. The goals of education at primary level are: Education for Universal access, minimising the wastage and stagnation, quality and equality of education, Universalisation of Elementary Education, making socially useful adults, functionality of education, making children attain atleast Minimum Levels of Learning in all subjects, reciprocal participation of community and students etc. The teacher should have sufficient knowledge regarding aims and objectives of the subject he teachers in the class and before knowing the learning out comes of teaching and the change of behaviour that is expected of a pupil, the aims and objectives should be fixed with the child becoming the centre of teaching.

Behaviours observed under this competency are

a. The teacher makes the children attain the optimum levels of teaching.

b. The teacher engages the children in activities like preparing the charts, clay models and other aids so that the three domains are achieved.

15. The teacher should have lesson planning skill and instructional management. (please refer to table no. 4.15)

Till very recently the teacher used to prepare lessons faithfully adhering to the Herbartian steps. While it is necessary to take advantage of the good points in the Herbartian steps, other factors such as the pupil's preparedness towards learning etc. have also to be kept in mind during lesson plan preparation.

Now a lesson is known as a teaching-learning situation as the importance enjoyed by the teacher is shared by both the teacher and the child, in most cases the importance is shifted to the child. The child takes initiative and the teacher may or may not remain even in the back ground. This has got deep significance.

While planning, teacher should keep in mind three major factors viz. i) what he/she wants to accomplish by teaching ii) teacher-learning processes and iii) what happens as a result of learning i.e., 'goals and outcome'. The teacher, for example, should formulate the specific objectives of the lesson, subject and pupils. In formulating the objectives, attention should be focussed on the probable change of the behaviour that will occur in the pupil as a result of learning. The outcomes that a teacher would expect after exposing the pupils to educational experience are: development of skills, development of knowledge, change or acquisition of values and attitudes and development of new interests. Lesson planning helps the teacher to steer his way through teaching-learning process to reach the desired goal.

Instructional management is the organising and controlling of a situation or incident which the teacher encounters in a classroom while interacting with the pupils. It has two broad components.

1. Expertise in planning for instruction which includes planning of a lesson with proper aims and objectives and fixing the learning outcomes and change of behaviour of a pupil through this planning.

2. Expertise in delivering instruction includes developing skills, attitudes, interests in pupils by proper method of teaching and various techniques that are involved in class room instruction.

Instructional Management also involves stages like (1) structuring, (2) modeling, (3) coaching, (4) fading, and (5) evaluation.

Structuring involves lesson planning skill like formulation of aims and objectives etc. Modeling involves the teacher acting as a model to develop a particular skill in the student like drawing a line and learning Geometry. The teacher draws pictures of triangles, squares, circles etc. and the students learn to perform the same by observing the teacher while the teacher shows the skill on the black board or using some other object and acting as a model. In coaching the teacher may hold the student's hand and make him draw a circle or a square or some other figure. Fading involves the withdrawl of support from the teacher and it expects the student to exhibit the skill on his own which he had learnt earlier from the teacher. Finally in evaluation the teacher corrects the errors committed by the student and knows how far he has learnt the skill.

Behaviours observed under this competency are

a. The teacher plans the lesson with clarity including what to teach; time allotment for a period of 30 or 45 mts.

b. The teacher plans with easy-moderate-difficult examples to meet the needs of all the students in the class.

EMPOWERING MANAGERIAL RELATED COMPETENCIES

Under managerial related competencies there are seven competencies (please refer to table no. 4.15). Managerial related competencies are useful for a teacher to deal effectively the classroom administration like maintaining discipline in the class room, motivating pupils to learn, developing easy and original innovative methods etc. To achieve the managerial related competencies the teacher should be a resourceful, hardworking, individual.

Managerial competencies are crucial now-a-days for the teacher as the demand for these competencies is even more these days since the teacher has to equip himself/herself with these competencies to accord with the changing needs of the pupils. The following paragraphs give complete information regarding the competencies (seven) that come under this managerial related competencies and the ways and the means suggested by the researchers to empower these competencies in teachers. Along with these are given the techniques administered by the researchers to empower each competency separately.

1. Means and ways of empowering competency no.1

The teacher should be everready to learn things and constantly augment his/her knowledge base.

The researchers have made an attempt to empower the above competency using SEMINAR and DISCUSSION techniques. The manner by which it had been done and the means and ways of administering the technique had been explained in the following paragraphs.

To empower the competency mentioned above all the 15 trainees were asked to present papers on various 'Latest techniques of teaching' and 'Educational technology and its application in teaching' in the form of a seminar. The trainees presented papers on various teaching skills to teach different subjects like Mathematics, Sciences and languages. The seminar also yielded a number of latest techniques in analysing classroom communication using Flander's system of International Analysis, improving teacher's skills through micro-teaching, use of programmed learning to learn the content by self-pace, computers and its uses in education etc.

Later the issues presented in the papers were put to discussion and from the material collected on latest techniques, 'Educational technology and its application the interest and zeal of trainees to learn new things to increase their knowledge was made to be empowered by the researchers.

2. Means and ways of empowering competency no.2

The teacher should realise the relevance and significance of teaching.

The researchers tried to empower the above competency using SEMINAR and DISCUSSION techniques.

The researchers asked the trainees to present papers on 'Environmental protection' 'Spread of diseases and their control' to find out how could they realise the relevance of teaching. The trainees presented papers on the topics and they were asked to explain how environment can be protected. In discussion session the various ways of protecting environment were discussed. Similarly the measures to be adopted to control the spread of diseases like malaria and cholera were also discussed. The sensitive areas which are prone to spread these diseases and the incidents like floods and other natural calamities, the erroneous ways of living which lead to the spread of diseases etc. were put to discussion and to ways of preventing the diseases were also discussed.

From the discussions of the trainees on the issues mentioned above, the researchers could know if the teachers could realise the relevance of the subjects they teach and significance of teaching and thus tried to empower the competency in teachers.

3. Means and ways of empowering competency no.3

The teacher should motivate pupils and incite interest in them to learn.

The researchers tried to empower the above competency using 'ROLE-PLAY' and 'OBSERVATION' techniques.

The researchers believe and feel that an intrinsically motivated teacher can in turn incite interest in pupils to learn. Intrinsic motivation is nurtured and developed when the needs of persons are fulfilled. Psychological needs like 'self-esteem', 'need for recognition', 'need for belongingness' etc. are to be fulfilled and when these are fulfilled, chances will be more for person to become intrinsically motivated. Inorder to findout the intrinsic motivation of the trainees the trainees were asked to 'ROLE-PLAY' the roles of incharges of various clubs. The trainee who is interested in painting was assigned to play the role of 'incharge' of Drawing club'. The trainee who is interested in sports was given the role of "sports' incharge". Similarly trainees were given to play the roles of supervising various clubs like 'Mathematics club', 'social studies club', 'little doctors' club', 'care and share' club', etc., depending upon their interest and aptitude. Since all the trainees were assigned the roles that are in consonance with their interests they derive maximum job satisfaction in the roles they played with total involvement in the work. The trainees also observed other teachers while they guide others and learnt the skills like communication skills, drawing skills, managerial skills, etc. by observing the interests of fellow teachers at work and thus the teachers tried to grow in their profession.

4. Means and ways of empowering competency no.4

The teacher should maintain discipline in the class-room to facilitate smooth instruction.

The researchers tried to empower the above competency using 'ROLE-PLAY' and 'OBSERVATION' techniques.

The researchers have played the role of a teacher in which teacher's role as a facilitator was attempted by establishing rapport with students (trainees playing the roles of students) rather than the role of a authoritarian who dominates the students by creating a tense climate in the class room. On the other hand the class room climate of a facilitator who inculcates self-discipline in students by understanding pupils academic problems, personal needs, interests were made to be observed by the trainees and they were made to know the difference of two types of class room atmosphere.

Having been motivated thus, the trainees were encouraged to continue the role of facilitation with more attachment to the students resulting in more disciplined classroom atmosphere.

5. Means and ways of empowering competency no.5

The teacher should be a resourceful person.

The researchers tried to empower the above competency using SYMPOSIUM and DISCUSSION techniques.

To empower the above competency, a symposium was conducted on 'privatisation of education', a topic which was found to be the common interest to the group after enquiring the trainees. Each one of the trainees were asked to speak on the topic for 15 minutes which was followed by discussion among the trainees. Intermittently, the researchers referred to the talk of the teachers and asked them about the pros and cons of their views and gave sufficient time to defend their talk by obtaining information from other sources also like obtaining information from books by visiting a library, by discussions with other teachers, by obtaining newspaper cuttings, etc., which directly help the teachers to become resourceful persons.

With this the teachers are expected to defend their talk presented in the symposium in respect of the common topic which they had delivered earlier for 15 minutes. Thus the researchers tried to make the trainees resourceful persons through which they can guide their students when the occasion arises.

6. Means and ways of empowering competency no.6

The teacher should be hardworking.

The researchers used to seminar and discussion techniques for empowering the above competency.

To empower the competency the researchers requested the teachers to list down the material they had collected regarding the various roles they had played earlier for motivating pupils and incite interest in them to learn (competency no. 3 in table 4.15) such as the incharges of "drawing club", "sports club", "Mathematics club" etc. The teachers were also requested to suggest innovative methods in teaching various subjects and also to suggest various means and ways of developing the spontaneity and creativity in pupils by way of various other activities, apart from conducting clubs. When teachers engaged themselves in planning the activities and gathering information that is useful for students, it makes teachers work hard and thus they can become hardworking individuals. Thus the researchers tried to empower hardworking competency teachers.

7. Means and ways of empowering competency no. 7

The teacher should develop easy, original and innovative methods to aid instruction.

The researchers made an attempt to empower the above competency using BRAINSTORMING, MODELING and OBSERVATION techniques.

First a brainstorming session was organised by the researchers with fifteen trainees for 20 minutes duration each in which various innovative methods and easy methods to teach children were brought out. This brainstorming session was conducted three times with fifteen teachers and the novel, innovative ideas, methods given by teachers were later analysed and evaluated carefully.

Through modeling technique the researchers have demonstrated some innovative methods to teach functional grammar, vocabulary and formation of sentences etc. in English using flash cards. Similarly some easy methods to teach additions, conservation of numbers, counting etc. in Mathematics was shown to them.

The trainees observed the techniques and methods given by the researchers, similarly other teachers were also made to observe some of the novel ideas given by the trainees in this session.

EMPOWERING VALUE RELATED COMPETENCIES

There are three competencies in the value related competency group. The techniques adopted for empowering the competencies are observation and role-play. Though it is difficult to empower values such as love, honesty, sincerity in teachers as they already form certain ethics and principles in their life and already they have imbibed values for themselves. It is easier to inculcate moral values in children as they do not form any opinions and attitudes in their minds in that age.

However, the researchers made an attempt to empower these values in teachers by using role-play and observation techniques the details of which are given in the succeeding pages.

Means and ways of empowering competency no. 8

The teacher should be honest and sincere.

Honesty is the clear conscience "before myself and before my fellow human beings". Honesty is the awareness of what is right and appropriate in one's role, one's behaviour and one's relationship. For example, the teacher who exactly arrives in time to school and leaves the campus doesn't necessarily imply honesty on his part. The teacher should continuously apply the principles which work at best for his students, for himself/herself and society and ethics and values which make class room functional and useful. When there is say a word of praise from others this works as tremendous incentive and boosts up his/her belief in honesty and sincerity.

The researchers have tried to empower the above competency using 'role-play' technique. The trainees were asked to play the role of a student and the researcher as a teacher. The researchers while teaching a lesson in the classroom drops his money purse intentionally. A trainee who acts as the student picks it up and gives it to the teacher. (researcher) The teacher appreciates the sincere gesture of the student by saying "you have helped me a lot", "you are a sincere person", etc., which act as positive reinforces for the student and drive the student to repeat the benevolent and sincere acts again and .again.

In another situation all the 15 trainees were assigned the roles of passengers travelling in a train. A passenger (researcher) gets down on a station but forgets to take his suitcase along with him. After some days a stranger meets the passenger (researcher) and returns the bag. The fellow passenger adds that he had found the address of the person in the suitcase and other important certificates in it. Knowing that how important they are, he came all the way to return it. The researcher expresses his gratefulness by saying "I am really indebted to you", "you are a God sent person", etc., words and cordially invites the person to have dinner with his family members and asks him to spend two days with the family members.

The way the researcher responded to the kind gesture of the fellow passenger and treating him with all gratitude and love act as positive reinforcers and makes the other person repeat such deeds in future. This positive reinforcers if repeatedly given in the person who show acts of honesty and sincerity, they can drive the fellows to become sincere and honest and thus repeat their sincere gestures again and again.

The researchers feel that instead of rebuking the student who fares a poor show in the examination, a word of praise or encouragement should be given if he shows a better performance. Similarly, while valuing the answer scripts of the students who are backward in studies the answers which are written correctly by them are to be highlighted by saying ""If you work little harder and put your efforts better, you can get good marks" etc. Similarly, the student who returns a pen or money lost by his fellow classmates should be given due encouragement in the classroom and the late-comer who usually arrives late should be given a word of praise if he arrives in time occasionally and should be made to realise the importance of being honest and sincere.

The researchers however, feel that A MORE COMPREHENSIVE PROCEDURE SHOULD BE ADOPTED TO EVALUATE SINCERITY AND HONESTY AND OTHER VALUES IN TEACHERS and they should be inculcated at the early stages of learning (between 5 to 11 years of age) in children.

The attempt made by the researchers to empower the above competency is not exhaustive, and the researchers feel that THE ABOVE COMPETENCY WAS NOT PROPERLY EVALUATED IN TEACHERS, although sincere attempts had been made to inculcate values in teachers. However, the researchers feel that a more comprehensive and genuine paradigm should be designed to inculcate the values such as honesty, sincerity, love, altruism, etc., in teachers as well as in children. Some activities to inculcate values such as altruism, affection, friendliness, in children are given by the researchers in the following pages under the title "Means and ways of empowering competency no. 10". (The teacher should develop moral values in children by giving striking examples from real life situations).

Means and ways of empowering competency no. 9

The teacher should love his/her profession.

The researchers tried to empower the above competency using 'role-play' technique.

The investigators have found out the interests hobbies, and attitudes of the trainees and accordingly they were asked to play the roles which are in consonance with their interests and likings. An artificial situation of a school was created and the trainees were asked to perform the roles which are in agreement with their interests. For, eg. the trainees who love books and interested in reading was assigned to play the role of a 'librarian' of the school. Similarly, the trainee who loves sports and games was assigned the role of a 'drill master' and the trainee who has interest in drawing and painting was assigned the role of an 'art teacher' and so on. The trainee inorder to enjoy his/her role which is in consonance with his interest, zeal and attitudes had exhibited a positive trend in attending the institution. Moreover, they derive maximum satisfaction and develop love and liking towards the job entrusted to them.

Thus, the researchers tried to empower the competency in teachers by using the above techniques.

Means and ways of empowering competency no. 10

The teacher should develop moral values in children by giving striking examples from real life situations.

The teacher can inculcate values such as honesty, sincerity, kindness, sympathy by giving a number of examples from real life.

The researchers tried to empower the above competency using role-play and observation technique. First the researchers tried the trainees to inculcate sympathy in them. Sympathy covers the aspects of 'capacity for being simultaneously affected with the same feeling as another', 'tendency to share another person's emotion', and 'mental participation with another in his trouble'.

For internalising 'sympathy' the activity planned is as follows.

The trainees were asked to play the roles of students and to form pairs. One in each pair was blind-folded and each pair was asked to walk through a series of obstacles like a ditch, tree or an overhanging branch with the partner who can see, leading. Since obstacles were not available, these were created with marks on the ground, posting trainees to be trees and using furniture. The partner who leads was asked to do so without talking, by taking the hand of his blind folded partner and make him feel the obstacles and difficulties the blind face in the daily life situations. This helps the trainees to develop sympathy in trainees. (students).

After a while, the roles in each pair was reversed and the same activity was conducted with five pairs of trainees. It was repeated for two days.

This activity of leading the blind involves 'capacity for being simultaneously affected with the same feeling as another' at the time of reversing the roles, where the trainee who led his blind-folded later, whereas 'tendency to share another person's emotion' at the time of feeling pain due to obstructions or falling', and 'mental preparation with another in his trouble' when the trainee who was leading interacts and guides the blind folded. Thus the researchers tried to develop 'sympathy' in trainees by this activity.

The researchers have also suggested some more activities for teachers to try them on their students to inculcate values such as 'affection' and 'altruism' in students.

To develop 'affection' which is showing or expressing kind feeling the activity planned to be introduced in the classroom is as follows.

Students are divided into two groups -A and B. In the role play, the students of group B, are asked to scratch the back and move a rubber lizard on the hands of group A members. The students feel the pinch and shout. At the juncture, the teacher poses a question as to what a tree feels when a squirrel runs up the trunk and when it is cut. Students of group A, having felt a strange feeling, answer that, the tree feels the scratching and hurt.

Next time, the roles of groups A and B are reversed.

Thus, the students understood and internalise that the plants and animals are living things like human beings and shouldn't be harmed. This activity develops affection towards other living things.

Similarly 'altruism' can be developed in students by the following activity.

The aspect covered in altruism are 'selfishness' and happiness of others first. To inculcate 'altruism' the following activities are planned.

1. A two weeks old pup is given to each of the two groups of students. They nurture the pups with the food they bring to school.

After three months, the nurturing of two pups is evaluated and the class which reared the pup to a healthy one is reinforced. The healthy pup received more attention, care and food, because of the unselfishness of the students.

Further, the reinforcement of one class by the teacher enables the students of other group to review their behaviour, and they will try to be unselfish in future.

The principle of considering the well-being and happiness of others first can be developed in the following manner.

During a potluck lunch session, teacher asks the children to give food stuffs, first to the neighbours and then feed themselves. In simple terms "Athidhi Devo Bhavah".

This activity is repeated, for the children to internalise the aspect of 'considering the well-being and happiness of others first.

These activities develop altruism in the students.

EMPOWERING PUPIL RELATED COMPETENCIES

Under pupil related competency group there are three competencies. Pupil related competencies include the attitude of teachers that has to be developed towards pupils these days by having a better rapport with them. The teachers should develop such a personality themselves so as to make pupils imbibe it and thus inspire them with their teaching and other characteristics. Drawing out the best talents that are innate in pupils is also the duty of a teacher. So, the researchers tried to empower these competencies in teachers so that pupils also will be benefited from the personality of the teacher.

Means and ways of empowering competency no.11

The teacher should be in intimate contact with students and be friendly with them. (please refer to table no. 4.15)

The researchers tried to empower the above competency by ROLE-PLAY and OBSERVATION techniques.

One of the teachers played the role of a teacher in which teacher's role as a friend, guide and intimate person to students (trainees playing the roles of students) was attempted and the academic problems, personal problems of students were known individually by spending some time with each student. The researcher remained friendly with students to remove the initial inhibition and fear complexes generally children develop in their minds towards the teacher. The trainees were made to know the difference between a friendly teacher who acts as a guide and friend with the children which resulted in more and more involvement of children and teacher in teaching learning process and which facilitated the children to clarify their doubts in a better way and which finally resulted in better motivation of children to attend the class etc. and the teacher who maintains an air of superiority and autocratic in his attitude towards children thus developing a fear complex in children was demonstrated by the researcher and the teachers were thus motivated to be more friendly with children.

The teachers after having been thus motivated were asked to adapt a friendly attitude with the children. Thus by observing the researcher the trainees developed various ways of establishing more rapport with students.

Means and ways of empowering competency no. 12

The teacher should stimulate, impress and inspire students not only by his/her teaching but by his/her personality also. (please refer to table no. 4.15)

The researchers tried to empower this competency using "MODELING" and "OBSERVATION" techniques.

The researchers used 'modeling' technique and demonstrated how to avoid monotony in the classroom while communicating with children. Certain humorous jokes, questions from the side of the pupils were encouraged by making the trainees ask questions and by answering them to their satisfaction. The teacher using 'sense of humour' in some cases of pupils indulging in mischievous acts and children asking silly questions were demonstrated by one of the researchers through 'modeling' technique. The trainees 'observed' the researcher while engaging the class and they were made to realise the ways by which they can inspire students by their teaching and personality. The trainees were also made to observe that along with teaching some other gestures like pleasant manners, habits and approaches from the side of a teacher can make pupils 'feel and 'develop' all admiration, adoration and reverence for that teacher.

Here are some suggestions for the teacher to impress the pupils:

1. Always use good encouraging language when a student does some good work. For example returning the money or a pen he/she found to the teacher.
2. Avoid using unparliamentary language.
3. Always control the emotions.
4. Don't give excessive physical punishments to pupils.
5. Don't show favour or partiality to a particular student.
6. Be punctual and regular to class.
7. Don't indulge in excessive talk with the pupils other than teaching.

8. The teacher should always appear neat and be careful about his/her dress.

Means and ways of empowering competency no. 13

The teacher should identify the latent talents in students and try to draw out the best in them. (please refer to table no. 4.15)

The researchers tried to empower the above competency using, OBSERVATION and MICRO-TEACHING techniques and DISCUSSION.

The trainees were requested to conduct with students atleast once in a week a totally democratic flexible discussion on the day-to-day life events and it was made to be explicit in students and they should be made to exhibit their inherent talents through various forms like art, dance, painting, reading, writing etc.

The trainees were asked to observe the students while they were continuing the discussion and the latent talents which they exhibit during the discussion like oratory skills, communication skills, etc. Similarly painting skills, music skills, etc., were to be developed by providing opportunities for them on children's day, Independence day, etc.

The researchers used micro-teaching technique through which the skill of probing questions and answer giving was accomplished the details of which are given in this chapter under the title "further suggestions for nurturing the competencies in teachers".

EMPOWERING CURRICULUM RELATED COMPETENCIES

Under curriculum related competency group there are two competencies. The first competency emphasizes that the teacher should know the aims, objectives of teaching the subject which covers the aspects of preparing aims and objectives from the pupil point of view. The second competency deals with lesson planning skill and instructional management which covers the aspects communication skills, skills of preparing a lesson plan, skills of probing questions etc.

Means and ways of empowering competency no. 14

The teacher should know the aim, goal and objectives of teaching the subject. (please refer to table 4.15)

The researchers tried to empower the above competency using SEMINAR and DISCUSSION techniques.

The researchers have conducted a seminar on realising objectives with pupils 'involvement' and the teachers were requested to frame aims and objectives and realising them with emphasis on making pupils achieve optimum levels of learning with more involvement of pupils in preparing models, charts and other teaching aids and thus making teaching more effective. Also more attention was focused on the behaviour that will occur in pupils as a result of learning and outcomes the teacher would expect after exposing the pupils to educational experience are: development of skills, acquisition or change of values and attitudes and new interests. The aims, objectives should help the teacher to steer this way to reach the desired goal.

The issues were then put to discussion and the researchers noted down the outcomes and some more suggestions were given to trainees regarding writing lesson plans. Some more details of writing lesson plans are given under the title "further suggestions for nurturing the competencies in teachers".

Means and ways of empowering competency no. 15

The teacher should have lesson planning skill and instructional management. (please refer to table no. 4. 15)

The researchers made an attempt to empower the above competency using OBSERVATION, DISCUSSION, MODELING and MICRO-TEACHING techniques.

The trainees were asked to prepare lesson plans in their respective subjects which they teach in their colleges for students. The trainees prepared lesson plans by discussing with other teachers and by observing other teachers who engaged in planning a lesson. During the lesson plan preparation the researchers, asked the trainees to give emphasis on factors such as pupils' preparedness towards learning, teaching-learning situation enjoyed by both teacher and child, and the shift of importance from teacher to child in teaching-learning situation etc. inaddition to prepare the lesson using Herbartian steps. The researchers thus tried to develop the lesson planning skill in teachers.

For empowering instructional management skill the researchers used micro-teaching and modeling techniques and tried to develop skills involved instructional management like communication skills, skills related to classroom management, skill of probing questions, etc.

Some more details regarding 'instructional management' are given under the title 'Further suggestions for nurturing the competencies in teachers' in chapter IV.

CLASSROOM OBSERVATIONS OF TEACHERS MADE BY THE RESEARCHERS AFTER THE ADMINISTRATION OF TECHNIQUES FOR EMPOWERMENT

After the completion of training for a period of four weeks, the researchers made an attempt to find out the effect of training in teachers. The researchers wanted to fund out to what extent the teachers who were given training for empowerment of competencies could incorporate these techniques of training in their teaching and put them in practice in their daily classroom teaching. To know the extent of empowerment of competencies, in teachers, the researcher has made observations of the teachers in the class room. The investigators have observed three classes for every teacher while the teachers were engaging their classes. The scoring procedure adopted by the researcher was same as explained earlier in this chapter before the administration of techniques has detailed in 4.12.1. For every teacher, the researchers noted down the post-test scores by awarding a score of '0' if the behaviour is not observed at all in the class room and 'I' if the behaviour is observed one time in the classroom or expressed by the teacher one time during the classroom instruction. Similarly a score of '2' is awarded if the behaviour is expressed two times by the teacher in the class room and a score of '3' if the behaviour is expressed 3 or more times. Accordingly the degree of empowerment is termed as "Not existing." "Trace", "Satisfactory" and "Sufficient". The researchers observed carefully every teacher's classroom instruction and awarded marks by following the scoring system mentioned above. The behaviours expressed by the teachers and the pre-test and post-test scores for fifteen teachers are given in the tables 4.16 to 4.30. For the sake of providing convenience and to avoid unnecessary confusion for the reader, the researchers have listed out only those behaviours and competencies for which the pre-test scores were either '0' or '1'. The observations made by the researchers are based on the concept that how far the teachers could incorporate the competencies in their daily classroom teaching after having incorporated the means and methods suggested by the researchers to empower the competencies.

The details of the pre-test and post-test scores of the fifteen teachers for the 15 most essential competencies with the behaviours expressed by the teachers for each competency are given in the following tables 4.16 to 4.30. Separate tables are given for all the 15 teachers for the convenience of the reader to show the pre-test and post-test scores and the averages of the scores and analysis regarding the degree of empowerment is carried out basing on the average post-test scores of the behaviours of the 15 teachers.

Abbreviations used are C1, C2, C3 and Avg which denote class no.1, class no.2, class no.3 and average of these three respectively. They are given immediately at end of each table.

Table 4.16.—Distribution of pre-test and post-test scores for most essential competencies observed with behaviours expressed by the teacher no. 1 in the class room.

Teacher	Competency statements	Behaviours expressed by the teacher	Class room observations of the teacher							
			PRE-TEST				POST-TEST			
			C-1	C-2	C-3	Avg.	C-1	C-2	C-3	Avg.
		The teacher								
Teacher No.1	1. The teacher should maintain discipline in class room to faci litate smooth instru- ction.	a) identifies with the class and never allows monotony to set in by quick shift of presentation.	0	0	1	0.33	2.0	2.0	3.0	2.3
		b) interacts freely with students and at the same time avoids giving excessive freedom by arresting deviated or irrelevant talks and questions of the students.	0	0	0	0	2.0	2.0	2.0	2.0

(Contd...)

1	2	3	4	5	6	7	8	9	10	11
	2. The teacher should be honest and sincere	a) discharges his/her duties with time sense like attending to school and taking classes regularly, and working for the academic and personality development of his/her pupils.	1.0	1.0	1.0	1.0	2.0	2.0	2.0	2.0
		b) attends to school work entrusted by developing his/her own resources and does it by using best capacities.	0	0	1.0	0.33	2.0	2.0	2.0	2.0
	3. The teacher should his/her profession.	A) works and teacher for extra time for the benefit of children even when the payment of remuneration for the extra work doesn't exist.	0	0	1.0	0.33	3.0	3.0	3.0	3.0
		b) attends to his school work on priority and then executes other responsibilities like family rituals, social functions etc.	0	0	1	0.33	3.0	3.0	3.0	3.0

	4. The teacher should realise the relevance and significance of teaching.	a) utilises all the available opportunities that are beneficial for the students viz., field trips, science fairs, sports and games.	0	0	0	0	3.0	3.0	3.0	3.0
		b) teaches all the units of syllabus without fail, if necessary by taking some special classes.	0	1.0	1.0	0.66	2.0	2.0	2.0	2.0
	5. The teacher should inspire, impress and stimulate students not only by his teaching but by his personality also.	a) believes and behaves with pleasant manners, habits and approaches.	0	0	1.0	0.33	2.0	2.0	2.0	2.0
		b) promotes pupils' curiosity and interest by clarifying their doubts with appreciation and always speaks good encouraging language.	0	0	1.0	0.33	3.0	3.0	3.0	3.0

(Contd...)

1	2	3	4	5	6	7	8	9	10	11
	6. The teacher should identify the latent talents in students and try to draw out the best in them.	a) encourages pupils to partici pate in drawing and painting competitions, elocution. essay writing, science fares etc. and gives sufficient guidance.	0	0	0	0	3.0	3.0	3.0	3.0
		b) maintains an anecdotal record and explores opportunities for his pupils.	1.0	1.0	1.0	1.0	2.0	2.0	2.0	2.0
	7. The teacher should develop easy original and innovative methods to aid instruction.	a) develops low cost aids by using the material available in school	1.0	1.0	1.0	1.0	2.0	2.0	2.0	2.0
		b) involves pupils in preparing teaching aids like charts, models to explain concepts relating to Mathematics, Sciences, Languages and arts.	0	0	0	0	2.0	2.0	2.0	2.0

	8. The teacher should be a resourceful person.	a) clarifies all the doubts of the students convincingly resulting in his students' happiness.	0	0	0	0	3.0	3.0	3.0	3.0
		b) voluntarily approaches the pupils to know their problems and tries to solve them convincingly.	0	0	0	0	2.0	2.0	2.0	2.0
	9. The teacher should the know the aims, goals and objectives of teaching the subject. but by his personality also.	a) makes children attain the optimum levels of teaching.	0	0	0	0	2.0	2.0	2.0	2.0
		b) engages students in activities like preparing the charts, clay models and other aids so that the three domains are achieved.	0	0	1	0.33	3.0	3.0	3.0	3.0

Where C1 = class one

C2 = class two

C3 = class three

Average gives the consistency of the teacher in expressing the bahaviours in the respective competency.

To avoid unnecessary repetition, of using the word teacher at the beginning of each behaviour in column 3, i.e., behaviours expressed by the teacher, the word 'teacher' has been given at the top of the table.

From the table no. 4.16, it could be found that the researchers have observed the pre-test and post-test scores of teacher at no.1 for nine competencies and eighteen behaviours expressed by the teacher in the classroom. By making comparisons of the pre-test and post-test scores as well as their averages of the behaviours, it is found that the average post-test scores for eleven behaviours is 2.0 for which the average pre-test scores were mostly 1.0 and less than 1.0. This means that for eleven behaviours out of eighteen, the teacher had exhibited that particular behaviour. It indicates that the teacher at no.1 had been empowered to a 'SATISFACTORY' degree.

Table 4.17.—Distribution of pre-test and post-test scores for most essential competencies observed with behaviours expressed by the teacher no. 2 in the class room

Teacher	Competency statements	Behaviours expressed by the teacher	Class room observations of the teacher							
			PRE-TEST				POST-TEST			
			C-1	C-2	C-3	Avg.	C-1	C-2	C-3	Avg.
		The teacher								
Teacher No.2	1. The teacher should maintain discipline in class room to facilitate smooth instruction	a) identifies with the class and never allows monotony to set inby quick shift of presentation.	0	0	1.0	0.33	2.0	2.0	2.0	2.0
		b) interacts freely with students and at the same time avoids giving excessive freedom by arresting deviated or irrelevant talks and questions of the students.	0	0	0	0	3.0	3.0	3.0	3.0

(Contd...)

1	2	3	4	5	6	7	8	9	10	11
	2. The teacher should be a resourceful person.	a) clarifies all the doubts of the students convincingly resulting in students' happiness.	0	0	0	0	3.0	3.0	3.0	3.0
		b) voluntarily approaches the pupils to know their problems and tries to solve them convincingly.	0	0	1.0	0.33	3.0	3.0	3.0	3.0
	3. The teacher must be hard working.	a) corrects the home work of the students by pin-pointing their mistakes.	0	0	0	0	3.0	3.0	3.0	3.0
		b) collects more information and material to make the lesson interesting and absorbing.	0	0	0	0	3.0	3.0	3.0	3.0
	4. The teacher should motivate pupils and incite interest in them to learn.	a) keeps on changing for novel and play-way methods to teach new concepts.	0	0	1.0	0.33	3.0	3.0	3.0	3.0
		b) tries to learn and prepare different types of charts and models to teach in the class; encourages them to succeed in various planned activities by assisting them.	1.0	1.0	1.0	1.0	3.0	3.0	3.0	3.0

	5. The teacher should be honest and sincere.	a) discharges his/her duties with time sense like attending to school regularly, taking classes regularly and working for the academic and personality development of pupils.	0	0	1.0	0.33	3.0	3.0	3.0	3.0
		b) attends to school work entrusted by developing his/her own resources and does it by using best capabilities.	0	0	0	0	2.0	2.0	2.0	2.0
	6. The teacher should inculcate moral values in children by giving striking examples from real life situations.	a) uses simulated situations and reinformces the experted behaviour when exhibited.	0	0	0	0	3.0	3.0	3.0	3.0
		b) organises small role-plays and dramas and makes the children to get the feeling of the 'roles' they enact.	0	0	0	0	3.0	3.0	3.0	3.0

(Contd...)

1	2	3	4	5	6	7	8	9	10	11
	7. The teacher should be in intimate contact with students and be friendly with them.	a) believes and behaves with pleasant manners, habits and approaches.	1.0	1.0	1.0	1.0	3.0	3.0	3.0	3.0
		b) doesn't snub or hurt the students by showing their defects; instead, encourages, helps and shows them the way in which they can overcome their lapses.	0	0	0	0	3.0	3.0	3.0	3.0
	8. The teacher should identify the latent talents in students and try out the best in them.	a) encourages the pupils to participate in drawing and painting competitions, elocution, debate, essay writing, science fares etc. and gives them sufficient guidance.	1.0	1.0	1.0	1.0	2.0	2.0	2.0	2.0
		b) maintains an anecdotal record and explores opportunities for his/her pupils.	0	0	0	0	3.0	3.0	3.0	3.0

Where C1 = class one

C2 = class two

C3 = class three

Average gives the consistency of the teacher in expressing the behaviours in the respective competency.

To avoid unnecessary repetition, of using the word teacher at the beginning of each behaviour in column 3, i.e., behaviours expressed by the teacher, the word 'teacher' has been given at the top of the table.

By making comparisons of the pre-test and post-test scores as well as their averages of the behaviours, it could be found, that average post-test- scores for eleven behaviours is 3.0 for which the average pretest scores were mostly 0 and less than 1.0. This means that for eleven behaviours out of sixteen, the teacher had exhibited that particular behaviour. It indicates that the teacher at no.2 had been empowered to a 'SUFFICIENT' degree.

Table 4.18—Distribution of pre-test and post-test scores for most essential competencies observed with behaviours expressed by the teacher no. 3 in the class room

Teacher	Competency statements	Behaviours expressed by the teacher	Class room observations of the teacher							
			PRE-TEST				POST-TEST			
			C-1	C-2	C-3	Avg.	C-1	C-2	C-3	Avg.
		The teacher								
Teacher No.3	1. The teacher should motivate pupils and incite interest in them to learn	a) keeps on changing for novel and playing methods to teach new concepts.	0	0	0	0	3.0	3.0	3.0	3.0
		b) tries to learn and prepare different types of charts and models to teach in the class; encourages them to succeed in various planned activities by assisting them.	1.10	1.0	1.0	1.0	2.0	2.0	2.0	2.0
	2. The teacher should be a resourceful person.	a) clarifies all the doubts of the students convincingly resulting in students' happiness.	1.01	1.0	1.0	1.0	3.0	3.0	3.0	3.0
		b) voluntarily approaches pupils to know their problems and tries to solve them.	0	0	0	0	3.0	3.0	3.0	3.0

	3. The teacher should develop easy original and innovative methods to aid instruction.	a) develops low cost aids by using the material available in school.	0	0	0	0	3.0	3.0	3.0	3.0
		b) involves pupils in preparing teaching aids like charts, models to explain concepts relating to science, mathematics etc.	0	0	0	0	2.0	2.0	3.0	2.3
	4. The teacher should inculcate moral values in children by giving striking examples from real life situations.	a) uses simulated situations and reinformces the experted behaviour when exhibited.	0	1.0	1.0	0.66	2.0	2.0	3.0	2.3
		b) organises small role-plays and dramas and makes the children to get the feeling of the 'roles' they enact.	0	0	0	0	3.0	3.0	3.0	3.0
	5. The teacher should identify the latent talents in students and try to draw out the best in them.	a) encourages the pupils to participate in drawing and painting competitions, elocution, debates, essay writing, science fairs etc. and gives them sufficient guidance.	0	0	0	0	3.0	3.0	3.0	3.0
		b) maintains an anecdotal record and explores opportunities for his/her pupils.	0	0	0	0	2.0	2.0	2.0	2.0

(Contd...)

1	2	3	4	5	6	7	8	9	10	11
	6. The teacher should be in intimate contact with students and be friendly with them.	a) creates a feeling of love and concern for them by attending individually to their academic and personal problems.	0	0	0	0	2.0	2.0	2.0	2.0
		b) doesn't snub or hurt the students by showing their defects; instead, encourages, helps and shows them the way in which they can overcome their lapses.	0	0	0	0	2.0	2.0	3.0	2.3
	7. The teacher must be hardworking.	a) corrects the home work of the students by pin-pointing their mistakes.	1.0	1.0	1.0	1.0	2.0	2.0	2.0	2.0
		b) collects more information and material to make the lesson interesting and absorbing.	1.0	1.0	1.0	1.0	2.0	2.0	2.0	2.0
	8. The teacher should know the aims, goals and objectives of teaching the subject.	a) makes children attain the optimum levels of teaching.	0	0	0	0	2.0	2.0	2.0	2.0
		b) engages students in activities like preparing the charts, clay models and other aids so that three domains are achieved.	0	0	0	0	2.0	2.0	3.0	2.3

	9. The teacher should have lesson planning skill and instructional management.	a) plans the lesson with clarity including what to teach, time allotment for a period of 30 or 45 mts.	0	0	0	0	3.0	3.0	3.0	3.0
		b) plans with easy-moderate-difficult examples to meet the needs of all students in the class.	0	0	0	0	3.0	3.0	3.0	3.0
	10. The teacher should be ready to learn new things and constantly augment his/her knowledge base.	a) regularly reads books pertaining to the subject, discusses important concepts will subject experts and senior teachers and increases his/her knowledge base.	0	0	0	0	2.0	2.0	2.0	2.0
		b) expresses willingness to attend workshop, inservice training programmes to know the latest techniques of teaching.	0	0	0	0	3.0	3.0	3.0	3.0

Where C1 = class one

C2 = class two

C3 = class three

Average gives the consistency of the teacher in expressing the behaviours in the respective competency.

To avoid unnecessary repetition, of using the word teacher at the beginning of each behaviour in column 3, i.e., behaviours expressed by the teacher, the word 'teacher' has been given at the top of the table.

From the table no. 4.18 it could be found that for teacher no. 3 ten competencies with twenty behaviours expressed in the class room with pre-test, post-test scores are given in the table. By making comparisions of pre-test and post-tes scores as well as their averges of behaviours it is found that average post-test scores for eleven behaviours is 2.0 or more than 2.0 for which the average pre-test scores were mostly 0. This means that for eleven behavious out of twenty, the teacher had exhibited that particular behaviour. It indicates that the teacher at no.3 had been empowered to a SATISFACTORY degree.

Table 4.19.—Distribution of pre-test and post-test scores for most essential competencies observed with behaviours expressed by the teacher no. 4 in the class room.

Teacher	Competency statements	Behaviours expressed by the teacher	Class room observations of the teacher							
			PRE-TEST				POST-TEST			
			C-1	C-2	C-3	Avg.	C-1	C-2	C-3	Avg.
Teacher No.4	1. The teacher should be everready to learn new things and constantly augment his knowledge base.	The teacher a) regularly reads books pertaining to the subject, discusses important concepts with subject experts and seniors to increase his/her knowledge base.	0	0	0	0	2.0	2.0	2.0	2.0
		b) expresses willingness to attend workshop inservice training programmes to know the latest techniques of teaching.	0	0	0	0	3.0	3.0	3.0	3.0

(Contd...)

1	2	3	4	5	6	7	8	9	10	11
	2. The teacher should develop easy, original and innovative methods to aid instruction.	a) develops low cost aids by using the material available in school	0	0	0	0	3.0	3.0	3.0	3.0
		b) involves pupils in preparing teaching aids like charts, models to explain concepts relating to mathematics, science, languages and arts.	0	0	1.0	0.33	3.0	3.0	3.0	3.0
	3. The teacher should inspire, impress and stimulate students not only by his teaching but by his/her personality also.	a) believes and behaves with pleasant manners, habits and approaches.	0	0	0	0	2.0	2.0	2.0	2.0
		b) promotes pupils curiosity and interest by clarifying their doubts with appreciation and always speaks good encouraging language.	0	0	0	0	3.0	3.0	3.0	3.0

	4. The teacher should identify the latent talents in students and try to drawout the best in them.	a) encourages pupils to participate in drawing and painting competitions, elocution debate, essay writing, science fares and gives them sufficient guidance.	0	0	1.0	0.33	3.0	3.0	3.0	3.0
		b) maintains an anecdotal record and explores opportunities for his/her pupils.	0	0	0	0	3.0	3.0	3.0	3.0
	5. The teacher must be sincere and honest.	a) discharges his/her duties with time sense like attending to school regularly, taking classes, regularly and working for the academic and personality.	0	0	0	0	3.0	3.0	3.0	3.0
		b) attends to school work entrusted by developing his/her own resources and does it by using best capabilities.	0	0	0	0	2.0	2.0	2.0	2.0

(Contd...)

1	2	3	4	5	6	7	8	9	10	11
	6. The teacher should inculcate moral values in children by giving striking examples from real life situations.	a) uses simulated situations and reinforces the experted behaviour when exhibited.	0	0	0	0	3.0	3.0	3.0	3.0
		b) organises small role-plays and dramas and makes the children get the feeling of the 'roles' they exact.	0	0	1	0.33	2.0	2.0	2.0	2.0
	7. The teacher must be hard working.	a) corrects the home work of the students by pin pointing their mistakes.	0	0	0	0	3.0	3.0	3.0	3.0
		b) collects more information and material to make the lesson interesting and absorbing.	0	0	0	0	3.0	3.0	3.0	3.0

	8. The teacher should motivate pupils and incite interest in them to learn.	a) keeps on changing for novel and play-way methods to teach new concepts.	0	0	0	0	3.0	3.0	3.0	3.0
		b) tries to learn and prepare different types of charts and models in the class; encourages them to succeed in various planned activities by assisting them.	0	0	0	0	3.0	3.0	3.0	3.0

Where C1 = class one

C2= class two

C3 = class three

Average gives the consistency of the teacher in expressing the behaviours in the respective competency.

To avoid unnecessary repetition, using the word teacher at the beginning of each behaviour in column 3, i.e. behaviours expressed by the teacher, the word 'teacher' has been given at the top of the table.

From the table no. 4.19 for teacher no.4, eight competencies and 16 behaviours expressed in the class room are observed and pre-test and post-test scores have been found out. By making comparisions of pre-test as well as post-test scores and their averages for the behaviours it could be found that average post-test scores for twelve behaviours is 3.0 for which the average pre-test scores for twelve behaviours is 3.0 for which the average pre-test scores were mostly 0. This means that for twelve beahviours out of sixteen, the teacher had exhibited that particular behaviour. It indicates that the teacher at no. 4 had been empowered to a SUFFICIENT degree.

Table 4.20.—Distribution of pre-test and post-test scores for most essential competencies observed with behaviours expressed by the teacher no. 5 in the class room.

Teacher	Competency statements	Behaviours expressed by the teacher	Class room observations of the teacher							
			PRE-TEST				POST-TEST			
			C-1	C-2	C-3	Avg.	C-1	C-2	C-3	Avg.
Teacher No.5	1. The teacher should be ever ready to learn new things and constantly augment his/her knowledge base.	The teacher a) regularly reads books pertaining to the subject discusses important concepts with subject experts and seniors to increase his/her knowledge base.	0	0	0	0	3.0	3.0	3.0	3.0
		b) expresses willingness to attend workshop, inservice training programmes to know the latest techniques of teaching.	0	0	0	0	3.0	3.0	3.0	3.0

(Contd...)

1	2	3	4	5	6	7	8	9	10	11
	2. The teacher should develop easy, original and innovative methods to aid instruction.	a) develops low cost aids by using the material available in school.	0	0	0	0	3.0	3.0	3.0	3.0
		b) involves pupils in preparing teaching aids like charts, models to explain concepts relating to mathematics, sciences, languages and arts.	0	0	0	0	2.0	2.0	2.0	2.0
	3. The teachers should inspire, impress and stimulate students not only by his/her teaching but by his/her personality also.	a) believes and behaves with pleasant manners, habits and approaches.	0	0	0	0	2.0	2.0	2.0	2.0
		b) promotes pupils' curiosity and interest by clarifying their doubts with appreciation and always speaks good encouraging language	0	0	0	0	2.0	2.0	2.0	2.0

	4. The teacher should identify the latent talents in students and try to drawout the best in them.	a) encourages pupils to participate in drawing and painting competitions, elocution, debate, essay writing, science fares and gives them sufficient guidance.	0	0	0	0	2.0	2.0	2.0	2.0
		b) maintains an anecdotal record and explores opportunities for his/her pupils.	0	0	1.0	0.33	3.0	3.0	3.0	3.0
	5. The teacher must be sincere and honest.	a) discharges his/her duties with time sense like attending to school regularly, taking classes regularly and working for the academic and personality development of the students	0	0	0	0	3.0	3.0	3.0	3.0
		b) attends to school work entrusted by developing his/her own resources and does it by using best capabilities.	0	0	0	0	3.0	3.0	3.0	3.0

(Contd...)

1	2	3	4	5	6	7	8	9	10	11
	6. The teacher should inculcate moral values in children by giving striking examples from real life situations.	a) uses simulated situations and reinforces the experted behaviour when exhibited.	0	0	1.0	0.33	2.0	2.0	2.0	2.0
		b) organises small role-plays and drams and makes the children to get the feeling of the 'roles' they exact.	0	0	0	0	3.0	3.0	3.0	3.0
	7. The teacher should be in intimate contact with students and be friendly with them.	a) creates a feeling of love and concern for them by attending individually to their academic and personal problems.	0	0	0	0	3.0	3.0	3.0	3.0
		b) doesn't snub or hurt the students by showing their defects; instead, encourages, helps and shows them the way in which they can overcome their lapses.	0	0	0	0	3.0	3.0	3.0	3.0

	8. The teacher must be hard working.	a) corrects the home work of the students by pin-pointing their mistakes.	0	0	0	0	3.0	3.0	3.0	3.0
		b) collects more information and material to make his/her lesson interesting and absorbing.	0	0	0	0	3.0	3.0	3.0	3.0

Where C1 = class one

C2 = class two

C3 = class three

Average gives the consistency of the teacher in expressing the behaviours in the respective competency.

To avoid unnecessary repetition, of using the word teacher at the beginning of each behaviour in column 3, i.e, behaviours expressed by the teacher, the word 'teacher' has been given at the top of the table.

From the table no. 4.20 for teacher no.7 it could be found that, eight competencies and 16 behaviours expressed in the class room are observed and pre-test and post-test scores and post test scores have been found out. By making comparisons of pre-test scores and their averages for the behaviours it could be that average post-test scores for eleven behaviours it is 3.0 for which average pre-test scores were mostly 0. This means that for eleven behaviours out of sixteen, the teacher had exhibited that particular behaviour. It indicates that the teacher at no. 5 had been empowered to a SUFFICIENT level.

Table 4.21.—Distribution of pre-test and post-test scores for most essential competencies observed with behaviours expressed by the teacher no. 6 in the class room.

Teacher	Competency statements	Behaviours expressed by the teacher	Class room observations of the teacher							
			PRE-TEST				POST-TEST			
			C-1	C-2	C-3	Avg.	C-1	C-2	C-3	Avg.
		The teacher								
Teacher No. 6	1. The teacher should motivate pupils and incite interest in them to learn.	a) keeps on changing for novel and play-way methods to teach new concepts.	0	0	0	0	2.0	2.0	2.0	2.0
		b) tries to learn and prepare different types of charts and models to teach in the class; encourages them to succeed in various planned activities by assisting them.	0	0	0	0	2.0	2.0	2.0	2.0

(Contd...)

1	2	3	4	5	6	7	8	9	10	11
	2. The teacher should maintain discipline in classroom to facilitate smooth instruction.	identifies with class and never allows monotony to set in by quick shift of presentation.	0	0	0	0	2.0	2.0	2.0	2.0
		b) interacts freely with students and at the same time avoids giving excessive freedom by arresting deviated or irrelevant talks and questions of the students.	0	0	1.0	0.33	3.0	3.0	3.0	3.0
	3. The teacher must be hard working.	a) corrects the home work of the students by pin-pointing their mistakes.	0	0	0	0	2.0	2.0	2.0	2.0
		b) collects more information and material to make his lesson interesting and absorbing.	0	0	1.0	0.33	2.0	2.0	2.0	2.0

	4. The teacher should develop easy, original and innovative methods to aid instruction.	a) develops low cost aids by using the material available in school.	0	0	0	0	2.0	2.0	2.0	2.0
		b) involves pupils in preparing teaching aids like charts, models to explain concepts relating to mathematics, sciences, languages and arts.	0	0	0	0	3.0	3.0	3.0	3.0
	5. The teacher should know the aims, goals and objectives of teaching the subject.	a) makes children attain the optimum levels of teaching.	0	0	0	0	2.0	2.0	2.0	2.0
		b) engages students in activities like preparing charts, clay models and other aids so that three domains are achieved.	0	0	0	0	2.0	2.0	2.0	2.0

(Contd...)

1	2	3	4	5	6	7	8	9	10	11
	6. The teacher should have lesson planning skill and instructional management.	a) plans the lesson with clarity including what to teach; time allotment for a period of 30 or 45 minutes.	0	0	0	0	3.0	3.0	3.0	3.0
		b) plans with easy-moderate difficult examples to met the needs of all students in the class.	0	0	1.0	0.33	3.0	3.0	3.0	3.0
	7. The teacher should inspire, impress and stimulate students not only by his teaching but personality also.	a) believes and behaves with pleasant manners, habits and approaches.	0	0	0	0	2.0	2.0	2.0	2.0
		b) promotes pupils' curiosity and interest by clarifying their doubts with appreciation and always speaks good encouraging language.	0	0	1.0	0.33	2.0	2.0	2.0	2.0

	8. The teacher should realise the relevance and significance of teaching.	a) utilises all the available opportunities that are beneficial for the students viz., field trips, science fares, sports and games.	0	0	0	0	2.0	2.0	2.0	2.0
		b) teaches all the units of syllabus without fail, if necessary by taking some special classes.	1.0	1.0	1.0	1.0	2.0	2.0	2.0	2.0

Where C1 = class one

C2 = class two

C3 = class three

Average give the consistency of the teacher in expressing the behaviours in the respective competency.

To avoid unnecessary repetition, of using the word teacher at the beginning of each behaviour in column 3, i.e., behaviours expressed by the teacher, the word 'teacher' has been given at the top of the table.

From the table no. 4.21 it could be found that for teacher no. 6, eight competencies and 16 behaviours expressed in the class room are observed and pre-test and past test scores have been found out. By making comparasions of pre-test and post-test scores and the averages for the behaviours it could be found that the average post-test scores for eleven behaviours are 2.0 for which the average pre-test scores were mostly 0 and less than 1.0. This means that for twelve behaviours out of sixteen, the teacher had exhibited that particular behaviour. It indicates that the teacher at no. 6 had been empowered to a SATISFACTORY level.

Table 4.22.—Distribution of pre-test and post-test scores for most essential competencies observed with behaviours expressed by the teacher no. 7 in the class room.

Teacher	Competency statements	Behaviours expressed by the teacher	Class room observations of the teacher							
			PRE-TEST				POST-TEST			
			C-1	C-2	C-3	Avg.	C-1	C-2	C-3	Avg.
		The teacher								
Teacher No.7	1. The teacher should know the aims, goals and objectives of teaching the subject.	a) makes children attain the optimum levels of teaching.	1.0	1.0	1.0	1.0	3.0	3.0	3.0	3.0
		b) engages students in activities preparing the charts, clay models and other aids so that three domains are achieved.	0	0	0	0	2.0	2.0	2.0	2.0

(Contd...)

1	2	3	4	5	6	7	8	9	10	11
	2. The teacher should motivate pupils and incite interest in them to learn.	a) keeps on changing for novel and play-way methods to teach new concepts.	1.0	1.0	1.0	1.0	2.0	2.0	2.0	2.0
		b) tries to learn and prepare different types of charts and models to teach in the class; encourages them to succeed in various planned activities by assisting them.	1.0	1.0	1.0	1.0	3.0	3.0	3.0	3.0
	3. The teacher should love his/her profession.	a) works and teachers for extra time for the benefit of children even when the payment of remuneration for extra time doesn't exist.	0	0	0	0	3.0	3.0	3.0	3.0
		b) attends to his/her school work in priority and then executes other responsibilities like family rituals, social functions etc.	0	0	0	0	3.0	3.0	3.0	3.0

	4. The teacher should maintain discipline in the classroom to facilitate smooth instruction.	a) identifies with the class and never allows monotony to set in by quick shift of presentation.	0	0	0	0	3.0	3.0	3.0	3.0
		b) interacts freely with students and at the same time avoids giving excessive freedom by arresting deviated or irrelevant talks and questions of the students.	0	0	0	0	3.0	3.0	3.0	3.0
	5. The teacher should realise the relevance and significance of teaching.	a) utilises all the available opportunities that are beneficial for students viz.,field trips, science fares, sports and games.	0	0	0	0	3.0	3.0	3.0	3.0
		b) teaches all the units of syllabus without fail, if necessary by taking some special classes.	0	0	0	0	2.0	2.0	2.0	2.0

(Contd...)

1	2	3	4	5	6	7	8	9	10	11
	6. The teacher should develop easy, original and innovative methods to aid instruction.	a) develops low cost aids by using the material available in school.	1	1	1	1.0	3.0	3.0	3.0	3.0
		b) involves pupils in preparing teaching aids like charts, models to explain concepts relating to mathematics, sciences, languages and arts.	1.0	1.0	1.0	1.0	2.0	2.0	2.0	2.0
	7.The teacher should inculcate moral values in children by giving striking examples from real life situations.	a) uses simulated situations and reinforces the experted behaviour when exhibited.	0	0	0	0	3.0	3.0	3.0	3.0
		b) organises small role-plays and dramas and makes the children to get the feeling of 'roles' they enact.	0	0	0	0	3.0	3.0	3.0	3.0

(Contd...)

	8. The teacher should be honest and sincere.	a) discharges his duties with time sense like attending to school regularly, taking classes regularly and working for the academic and personality development of his/her own pupils.	0	0	0	0	3.0	3.0	3.0	3.0
		b) attends to school work entrusted by developing his/her own resources and does it by using best capabilities	0	0	0	0	2.0	2.0	2.0	2.0

Where C1 = class one

C2 = class two

C3 = class three

Average gives the consistency of the teacher in expressing the behaviours in the respective competency.

To avoid unnecessary repetition, of using the word teacher at the beginning of each behaviour in column 3, i.e., behaviours expressed by the teacher, the word 'teacher' has been given at the top of the table.

From the table no. 4.22 it could be found that for teacher no.7, eight competencies and 16 behaviours expressed in the class room are observed and pre-test and post-test scores have been found out. By making comparasions of pre-test and post-test scores and the averages of behaviours it could be found out that for eleven behaviours the average post-test scores are 3.0 for which the average pre-test scores were mostly 0. This means that for eleven behaviours out of sixteen the teacher had exhibited that particular behaviour. It indicates that the teacher had been empowered to a SUFFICIENT degree.

Table 4.23.—Distribution of pre-test and post-test scores for most essential competencies observed with behaviours expressed by the teacher no. 8 in the class room

Teacher	Competency statements	Behaviours expressed by the teacher	Class room observations of the teacher							
			PRE-TEST				POST-TEST			
			C-1	C-2	C-3	Avg.	C-1	C-2	C-3	Avg.
Teacher No.8	1. The teacher should know the aims, goals and objectives of teaching the subject.	The teacher a) makes children attain the optimum levels of teaching.	1.0	1.0	1.0	1.0	3.0	3.0	3.0	3.0
		b) engages students in activities like preparing the charts, clay models and other aids so that three domains are achieved.	1.0	1.0	1.0	1.0	3.0	3.0	3.0	3.0

(Contd...)

1	2	3	4	5	6	7	8	9	10	11
	2. The teacher should love his/her profession.	a) works and teaches for extra time for the benefit of children even when the payment of remuneration for extra time doesn't exist.	0	0	0	0	2.0	2.0	2.0	2.0
		b) attends to his school work in priority and then executes other responsibilities like family rituals, social functions etc.	0	0	0	0	2.0	2.0	2.0	2.0
	3. The teacher should be a resourceful person.	a) clarifies all the doubts of the students convincingly resulting in his/her students' happiness.	0	0	0	0	3.0	3.0	3.0	3.0
		b) voluntarily approaches the pupils to know their problems and tries to solve them convincingly.	1.0	1.0	1.0	1.0	3.0	3.0	3.0	3.0

	4. The teacher should inculcate moral values in children by giving striking examples from real life situations.	a) uses simulated situations and reinforces the experted behaviour when exhibited.	0	0	1.0	0.33	3.0	3.0	3.0	3.0
		b) organises small role-plays and drams and makes the children get the feeling of 'roles' they enact.	0	0	1.0	0.33	3.0	3.0	3.0	3.0
	5. The teacher should inspire, impress and stimulate students not only by his/her teaching but by his/her personality also.	a) believes and behaves with pleasant manners, habits and approaches.	0	0	0	0.33	3.0	3.0	3.0	3.0
		b) promotes pupils' curiosity and interest by clarifying their doubts with appreciation and always speaks good encouraging language.	0	0	0	0	2.0	2.0	2.0	2.0

(Contd...)

1	2	3	4	5	6	7	8	9	10	11
	6. The teacher should realise the relevance and significance of teaching.	a) utilises all the available opportunities that are beneficial for students viz., field trips, science fares, sports and games.	0	0	0	0	2.0	2.0	2.0	2.0
		b) teaches all the units of syllabus without fail, if necessary by taking some special classes.	0	0	0	0	3.0	3.0	3.0	3.0
	7. The teacher should have lesson planning skill skill instructional management.	a) plans the lesson with clarity including what to teach; time allotment for a period of 30 or 45 minutes.	0	1.0	1.0	0.66	3.0	3.0	3.0	3.0
		b) plans with easy-moderate difficult examples to meet the needs of all students in the class.	0	1.0	1.0	0.66	3.0	3.0	3.0	3.0

Where C1 = class one

C2 = class two

C3 = class three

Average gives the consistency of the teacher in expressing the behaviours in the respective competency.

To avoid unnecessary repetition, of using the word teacher at the beginning of each behaviour in column 3, i.e., behaviours expressed by the teacher, the word 'teacher' has been given at the top of the table.

Table no. 4.23 gives information regarding seven competencies and fourteen behaviours expressed by the teacher no.8 with pre-test and post-test scores in the class room. By making comparisons of the pre-test and post-test scores the average post-test scores for 10 behaviours are 3.0. This means that for ten behaviours the teacher at no.8 had exhibited the particular behaviour. It indicates that the teacher had been empowered to a SUFFICIENT degree.

Table 4.24.—Distribution of pre-test and post-test scores for most essential competencies observed with behaviours expressed by the teacher no.9 in the class room.

Teacher	Competency statements	Behaviours expressed by the teacher	Class room observations of the teacher							
			PRE-TEST				POST-TEST			
			C-1	C-2	C-3	Avg.	C-1	C-2	C-3	Avg.
		The teacher								
Teacher No.9	1. The teacher should be honest and sincere.	a) discharges his/her duties with time sense like attending to school regularly, taking classes regularly and working for the academic and personality development of his/her pupils.	0	0	0	0	0	0	1.0	0.33
		b) attends to school work entrusted by developing his/her own resources and does it by using best capabilities.	0	0	0	0	0	1.0	1.0	0.66

	2. The teacher should develop easy, original and innovative methods to aid instruction.	a) develops low cost aids by using the material available in school.	0	0	0	0	0	0	1.0	0.33
		b) involves pupils in preparing teaching aids like charts, models, to explain concepts relating to mathematics, sciences, languages and arts.	0	0	0	0	0	0	0	0
	3. The teacher should maintain discipline in classroom to facilitate smooth instruction.	a) identifies with the class and never allows monotony to set in by quick shift of persentation.	0	0	0	0	0	0	1.0	0.33
		b) interacts freely with students and at the same time avoids giving excessive freedom by arresting deviated or irrelevent talks and questions of students.	0	0	0	0	1.0	1.0	1.0	1.0

(Contd...)

1	2	3	4	5	6	7	8	9	10	11
	4. The teacher should inspire, impress and stimulate students not only by his teaching but by his personality also.	a) believes and behaves with pleasant manners, habits and approaches.	0	0	0	0	0	0	1.0	0.33
		b) promotes pupils' curiosity and interest by clarifying their doubts with appreciation and always speaks good encouraging language.	0	0	0	0	0	0	1.0	0.33
	5. The teacher should be a resourceful person.	a) clarifies all the doubts of the students convingly resulting his his/her students' behaviour.	0	0	0	0	0	0	0	0
		b) voluntarily approaches the pupils to know their problems and tries to solve them convincingly.	0	1.0	1.0	0.66	0	1.0	1.0	0.66

	6. The teacher should motivate pupils and incite interest in them to learn.	a) keeps on changing for novel and play-way methods to teach new concepts.	0	0	1.0	0.33	0	1.0	1.0	0.66
		b) tries to learn and prepare different types of charts and models to teach in the class; encourages them to succeed in various planned activities by assisting them.	1.0	1.0	1.0	1.0	1.0	1.0	1.0	1.0
	7. The teacher should be ever-ready to learn new things and constantly augment his/her knowledge base.	a) regularly reads books pertaining to the subject, discusses important concepts with subject experts and seniors to increse his/her knowledge base.	0	0	0	0	0	0	0	0
		b) expresses willingness to attend workshop, inservice training programmes to know the latest techniques of teaching.	0	0	0	0	0	0	1.0	0.33

(Contd...)

1	2	3	4	5	6	7	8	9	10	11
	8. The teacher should maintain discipline in class room to facilitate smooth instruction	a) identifies wit the class and never allows monotony to set in by quick shift of presentation.	0	0	0	0	0	0	0	0
		b) interacts freely with students and at the same time avoids giving excessive freedom by arresting deviated or irrelevant talks and questions of the students.	0	0	0	0	0	0	0	0
	9. The teacher should be in intimate contact with students and be friendly with them.	a) creates a feeling of love and concern for them by attending individually to their academic and personal problems.	0	0	0	0	0	0	0	0
		b) doesn't snub or hurt the students by showing their defeats; instead, encourages helps and shows them the way in which they can overcome their lapses.	0	0	0	0	0	0	0	0

	10. The teacher should identify the latent talents in children and try to draw out the best in them.	a) encourages pupils to participate in drawing and painting competitions, elocution, debate, essay writing, science fares and gives them sufficient guidance.	0	0	1.0	0.33	0	0	1.0	0.33
		b) maintains an anecdotal record and explores opportunities for his/her pupils.	0	0	0	0	0	0	1.0	0.33
	11. The teacher should know the aims, goals and objectives of teaching the subject.	a) makes the children attain the optimum levels of teaching.	0	0	0	0	0	0	0	0
		b) engages students in activities like preparing the charts, clay models and other aids so that the three domains are achieved.	0	1.0	1.0	0.6	0	1.0	1.0	0.6

Where C1 = class one

C2 = class two

C3 = class three

Average gives the consistency of the teacher in expressing the behaviors in the respective competency.

To avoid unnecessary repetition, of using the word teacher at the beginning of each behaviour in column 3, i.e., behaviours expressed by the teacher, the word 'teacher' has been given at the top of the table.

From the table no. 4.24 it could be found that for teacher no. 9 the researchers have observed eleven competencies and twenty two behaviours expressed by the teacher in the class room. By comparing the pre-test and post-test score of the behaviours it is evident that empowerment was not at all encouraging for the teacher. The average post-test scores 0, 0.33 and 0.66 show that empowerment had not been done and encouraging. The teacher could not raise his competency except a behavior in competency no. 5 competency no. 6 two behaviours and a behaviour in competency no. 11 which indicates that no empowerment had been done in teacher at no.9.

Table 4.25.—Distribution of pre-test and post-test scores for most essential competencies observed with behaviours expressed by the teacher no. 10. in the class room

Teacher	Competency statements	Behaviours expressed by the teacher	Class room observations of the teacher							
			PRE-TEST				POST-TEST			
			C-1	C-2	C-3	Avg.	C-1	C-2	C-3	Avg.
		The teacher								
Teacher No.10	1. The teacher should inculcate moral values in children by giving striking examples from real life situations.	a) uses simulated situations and reinforces the experted behaviour when exhibited.	1.0	1.0	1.0	1.0	2.0	2.0	2.0	2.0
		b) organise small role-plays and dramas and makes the children to get the feeling of 'roles' they enact.	1.0	1.0	1.0	1.0	2.0	2.0	3.0	2.3

(Contd...)

1	2	3	4	5	6	7	8	9	10	11
	2. The teacher should develop easy, original and innovative methods to aid instruction.	a) develops low cost aids by using the materials available in school.	0	0	0	0	2.0	2.0	2.0	2.0
		b) involves pupils in preparing teaching aids like charts, models, to explain concepts relating to mathematics, sciences, languages and arts.	1.0	1.0	1.0	1.0	2.0	2.0	2.0	2.3
	3. The teacher should maintain discipline in class-room to facilitate smooth instruction.	a) identifies with the class and never allows monotony to set in by quick shift of presentation.	0	0	0	0	2.0	2.0	2.0	2.0
		b) interacts freely with students and at the same time avoids giving excessive freedom by arresting deviated or irrelevent talks and questions of students.	0	0	0	0	2.0	2.0	2.0	2.0

	4. The teacher should be a resourceful person.	a) clarifies all the doubts of the students convincingly resulting in his students' behaviour.	1.0	1.0	1.0	1.0	3.0	3.0	3.0	3.0
		b) voluntarily approaches the pupils to know their problems and tries to solve them convincingly.	1.0	1.0	1.0	1.0	3.0	3.0	3.0	3.0
	5. The teacher should love his profession. when the payment	a) works and teachers for extra time for the benefit of children even of remuneration for extra time doesn't exist.	0	1.0	1.0	0.66	2.0	2.0	2.0	2.0
		b) attends to his/her school work in priority and then executes other responsibilities like family rituals social functions etc.	0	1.0	1.0	0.66	2.0	2.0	2.0	2.0

(Contd...)

1	2	3	4	5	6	7	8	9	10	11
	6. The teacher should be ready to learn new things and constantly augment his/ her knowledge	a) regularly reads books pertaining to the subject, discusses important concepts with subject experts and seniors to increase his/her knowledge base.	0	0	1.0	0.33	2.0	2.0	2.0	2.0
		b) expresses willingness to attend workshop, inservice training programmes to know the latest techniques of teaching.	0	0	1.0	0.33	2.0	2.0	3.0	2.3
	7. The teacher should realise the reievance and significance of teaching.	a) utilises all the available opportunities that are beneficial for students viz., field trips, science fares, sports and games.	0	0	0	1.0	2.0	2.0	2.0	2.0
		b) teaches all the units of syllabus without fail, if necessary by taking some special classes.	1.0	1.0	1.0	1.0	2.0	2.0	2.0	2.0

	8. The teacher should be in intimate contact with students and be friendly with them.	a) creates a feeling of love and concern for them by attending individually to their academic and personal problems.	1.0	1.0	1.0	1.0	2.0	2.0	2.0	2.0
		b) doesn't snub or hurt the students by showing their defects; instead, encourages, helps and shows them the way in which they can over come their lapses.	0	0	1.0	0.33	2.0	2.0	2.0	2.0
	9. The teacher should identify the latent talents in students and try to draw out the best in them.	a) encourages pupils to participate in drawing and painting competitions, elocution, debate, essay writing, science fares and gives them sufficient guidance.	1.0	1.0	1.0	1.0	2.0	2.0	2.0	2.0-
		b) maintains an anecdotal record and explores opportunities for his/her pupils.	1.0	1.0	1.0	1.0	2.0	2.0	2.0	2.0

(Contd...)

1	2	3	4	5	6	7	8	9	10	11
	10. The teacher should have lesson planning skill and instructional management.	a) plans the lesson with clarity including what to teach, time allotment for a period of 30 or 45 minutes.	0	0	0	0	2.0	2.0	2.0	2.0
		b) plans with easy-moderate difficult examples to meet the needs of all the students in the class.	0	0	1.0	0.33	2.0	2.0	2.0	2.0

Where C1 =class one

C2 = class two

C3 =class three

Average gives the consistency of the teacher in expressing the baviours in the respective competency.

To avoid unnecessary repetition, of using the word teacher at the beginning of each behavior in column 3, i.e., behaviours expressed by the teacher, the word 'teacher' has been given at the top of the table.

From the table no. 4.25 for teacher no. 10 it could be found that a total number of ten competencies, and twenty behaviours expressed by the teacher in the class room are observed by the researchers. By making comparisons of the pre-test scores and post-test scores and their averages, it is found that for sixteen behaviours out of twenty for which the pre-test averages were mostly 1.0, the average post-test scores are 2.0. This means that for sixteen behaviours the teacher had exhibited that particular behaviour. It indicateds that the teacher at no. 10. had been empowered to a SATISFACTORY degree.

Table 2.26.—Distribution of pre-test and post-test scores for most essential competencies observed with behaviours expressed by the teacher no. 11 in the class room

Teacher	Competency statements	Behaviours expressed by the teacher	Class room observations of the teacher							
			PRE-TEST				POST-TEST			
			C-1	C-2	C-3	Avg.	C-1	C-2	C-3	Avg.
		The teacher								
Teacher No.11	1. The teacher should identify the latent talents in students and try to draw out the best in them.	a) encourages pupils to participate in drawing and painting competitions, elocution, debate, essay writing, science fares and gives them sufficient guidance.	0	0	1.0	0.33	3.0	3.0	3.0	3.0
		b) maintains an anecdotal record and explores opportunites for his/her pupils.	0	0	0	0	2.0	2.0	3.0	2.3

	2. The teacher must be hard working.	a) corrects the home work of the students by pin-pointing their mistakes.	1.0	1.0	1.0	1.0	3.0	3.0	3.0	3.0
		b) collects more information and material to make his/her lesson interesting and absorbing.	1.0	1.0	1.0	1.0	2.0	2.0	2.0	2.0
	3. The teacher should be a resourceful person.	a) clarifies all the doubts of the students convincingly resulting in their happiness.	1.0	1.0	1.0	1.0	2.0	2.0	3.0	2.3
		b) voluntarily approaches the pupils to know their problems and tries to solve them convincingly.	1.0	1.0	1.0	1.0	2.0	2.0	3.0	2.3

(Contd...)

1	2	3	4	5	6	7	8	9	10	11
	4. The teacher should be in intimate contact with students and be friendly with them.	a) creates a feeling of love and convern for them by attending individually to their academic and personal problems.	0	0	0	0	2.0	2.0	2.0	2.0
		b) doesn't snub or hurt the students by showing their defects; instead, encourages, helps and shows them the way in which they can overcome their lapses.	1.0	1.0	1.0	1.0	2.0	2.0	3.0	2.3
	5. The teacher should know the aims, goals and objectives of teaching the subject.	a) makes the children attain the optimum levels of teaching.	0	1.0	1.0	0.66	3.0	3.0	3.0	3.0
		b) engages students in activities like preparing the charts, clay models and other aids so that the three domains are achieved.	0	1.0	1.0	0.66	2.0	2.0	2.0	2.0

	6. The teacher should have lesson planning skill and instructional management.	a) plans the lesson with clarity including what to teach, time allotment for a period of 30 or 45 minutes.	0	0	0	0	2.0	2.0	2.0	2.0
		b) plans with easy-moderate difficult examples to meet the needs of all the students in the class.	0	0	0	0	2.0	2.0	2.0	2.0
	7. The teacher should maintain discipline in class-room to facilitate smooth instruction.	a) identifies with the class and never allows monotony to set in by quick shift of presentation.	0	0	0	0	2.0	2.0	2.0	2.0
		b) interacts freely with students and at the same time avoids giving excessive freedom by arresting deviated or irrelevant talks and questions of students.	0	0	1.0	0.3	2.0	2.0	2.0	2.0

Where C1 = class one

C2 = class two

C3 = class three

Average gives the consistency of the teacher in expressing the behaviours in the respective competency.

To avoid unnecessary repetition of using the word teacher at the beginning of each behaviour in column 3, i.e., behaviours expressed by the teacher, the word 'teacher' has been given at the top of the table.

From the table no. 4.26 for teacher no. 11 it could be found that a total number of even competencies, and fourteen behaviurs expressed by the teacher in the class room are observed by the researchers. By making comparisions of pre-test and post-test scores and their averages of behaviours, it is found that for eleven behaviours the average post-test scores are either 2.0 or more than 2.0. It means for eleven behaviours the teacher had exhibited that particular behaviour. It indicates that the teacher at number 11 had been empowered to a SATISFACTORY level.

Table 4.27.—Distribution of pre-test and post-test scores for most essential competencies observed with behaviours expressed by the teacher no.12 in the class room

Teacher	Competency statements	Behaviours expressed by the teacher	Class room observations of the teacher							
			PRE-TEST				POST-TEST			
			C-1	C-2	C-3	Avg.	C-1	C-2	C-3	Avg.
Teacher No.12	1. The teacher should motivate pupils and incite interest in them to learn.	The teacher a) keeps on changing for model and play-way methods to teach new concepts.	1.0	1.0	1.0	1.0	3.0	3.0	3.0	3.0
		b) tries to learn and prepare different types of charts and models to teach in the class; encourages them to succeed in various planned activities by assisting them	1.0	1.0	1.0	1.0	2.0	2.0	2.0	2.0

(Contd...)

1	2	3	4	5	6	7	8	9	10	11
	2. The teacher must be hard working.	a) corrects the home work of the students by pin-pointing their mistakes.	0	0	0	0	2.0	2.0	2.0	2.0
		b) collects more information and material to make his/her lesson interesting and absorbing.	1.0	1.0	1.0	1.0	2.0	2.0	2.0	2.0
	3. The teacher should be a resourceful person.	a) clarifies all the doubts of the students convincingly resulting in their happiness.	0	0	1.0	0.33	2.0	2.0	2.0	2.0
		b) voluntarily approaches the pupils to know their problems and tries to solve them convincingly.	0	0	1.0	0.33	2.0	2.0	2.0	2.0

	4. The teacher should inspire, impress and stimulate students not only by his/her teaching but by his/her personality also.	a) believes and beahves with pleasant manners, habits and approaches.	0	0	0	0	3.0	3.0	3.0	3.0
		b) promotes pupils curiosity and interest by clarifying their doubts with appreciation and always speaks good encouraging language.	0	0	0	0	3.0	3.0	3.0	3.0
	5. The teacher should know the aims, goals and objectives of teaching the subject.	a) makes the children attain the optimum levels of teaching.	0	0	0	0	3.0	3.0	3.0	3.0
		b) engages students in activities like preparing the charts, clay models and other aids so that the three domains are achieved.	0	0	1.0	0.33	3.0	3.0	3.0	3.0

(Contd...)

1	2	3	4	5	6	7	8	9	10	11
	6. The teacher should have lesson planning skill and instructional management.	a) plans the lesson with clarity including what to teach, time allotment for a period of 30 or 45 minutes.	1.0	1.0	1.0	1.0	3.0	3.0	3.0	3.0
		b) plans with easy-moderate difficult examples to meet the needs of all the students in the class.	0	0	1.0	0.33	3.0	3.0	3.0	3.0
	7. The teacher should develop easy, original and innovative methods to aid instruction.	a) develops low cost aids by using the material available in school.	0	0	0	0	3.0	3.0	3.0	3.0
		b) involves pupils in preparing teaching aids like charts, models to explain concepts relating to mathematics, sciences, languages and arts.	0	0	0	0	3.0	3.0	3.0	3.0

	8. The teacher should identify the latent talents in students and try to draw out the best in them.	a) encourages pupils to particiate in drawing and painting competitions, elocution, debate, essay writting, science fares and gives them sufficient guidance.	0	0	0	0	3.0	3.0	3.0	3.0
		b) maintains an anecdotal record and explores opportunities for his/her pupils.	0	0	0	0	2.0	2.0	2.0	2.0

Where C1 = class one

C2 = class two

C3 = class three

his/her Average give the consistency of the teacher in expressing the behaviours in the respective competency.

To avoid unnecessary repetition, of using the word teacher at the beginning of each behaviour in coloumn 3, i.e., behaviours expressed by the teacher, the word 'teacher' has been given at the top of the table.

From the table no. 4.27 for teacher no. 12 it could be found that a total number of eight competencies, and sixteen behaviours expressed by the teacher in the class room are observed by the researchers. After making pre-test and post-test comparisions and the averages of the behaviours it is found that for 10 behaviours the average post-test scores are 3.0 for which the pre-test scores either 0 or less than 0. This means that for 10 behaviours out of sixteen the teacher had exhibited that particular behaviour. It indicates that the teacher at no. 12 had been empowered to a SUFFICIENT degree.

Table 4.28—Distribution of pre-test and post-test scores for most essential competencies observed with behaviours expressed by the teacher no. 13 in the class room

Teacher	Competency statements	Behaviours expressed by the teacher	Class room observations of the teacher							
			PRE-TEST				POST-TEST			
			C-1	C-2	C-3	Avg.	C-1	C-2	C-3	Avg.
Teacher No.13	1. The teacher should develop easy, original and innovative metthods to aid instruction.	The teacher a) develops low cost aids by using the material available in school.	1.0	1.0	1.0	1.0	2.0	2.0	2.0	2.0
		b) involves pupils in preparing teaching aids like charts, models to explain concepts relating to mathematics, sciences, languages and arts.	0	0	0	0	3.0	3.0	3.0	3.0

(Contd...)

1	2	3	4	5	6	7	8	9	10	11
	2. The teacher should realise the relevance and significance of teaching.	a) utilises all the available opportunities that are beneficial for students viz., field trips, science fares, sports and games.	1.0	1.0	1.0	1.0	3.0	3.0	3.0	3.0
		b) teaches all the units of syllabus without fail, if necessary by taking some special classes.	1.0	1.0	1.0	1.0	3.0	3.0	3.0	3.0
	3. The teacher should be honest and sincere.	a) discharges his/her duties with time sense like attending to school regularly, talking classes regularly and working for the academic and personality development of his/her pupils.	1.0	1.0	1.0	1.0	2.0	2.0	2.0	2.0
		b) attends to school work entrusted by developing his/her own resources and does it by using best capabilities.	1.0	1.0	1.0	1.0	2.0	2.0	2.0	2.0

	4. The teacher should maintain discipline in classroom to facilitate smooth instruction.	a) identifies with the class and never allows monotony to set in by quick shift of presentation.	1.0	1.0	1.0	1.0	2.0	2.0	2.0	2.0
		b) interacts freely with students and at the same time avoids giving excessive freedom by arresting deviated or irrelevant talks and questions of students.	1.0	1.0	1.0	1.0	3.0	3.0	3.0	3.0
	5. The teacher should be ready to learn new things and constantly augment his/her knowledge base.	a) regularly reads books pertaining to the subject, discusses important concepts with subject experts and seniors to increase his/her knowledge base.	0	0	0	0	3.0	3.0	3.0	3.0
		b) expresses willingness to attend workshop, inservice training programmes to know the latest techniques of teaching.	1.0	1.0	1.0	1.0	3.0	3.0	3.0	3.0

(Contd...)

1	2	3	4	5	6	7	8	9	10	11
	6. The teacher should love his profession.	a) works and teaches for extra time for the benefit of children even when the payment of remuneration for extra time doesn't exist.	0	0	0	0	3.0	3.0	3.0	3.0
		b) attends to his school work in priority and then executes other responsibilities like family rituals, social functions etc.	1.0	1.0	1.0	1.0	2.0	2.0	2.0	2.0
	7. The teacher should inculcate moral values in children by giving striking examples from real life situations.	a) uses simulated situat ions and reinforces the experted behaviour when exhibited.	0	0	0	1.0	2.0	2.0	2.0	2.0
		b) organises small role-plays and dramas and makes the children to get the feeling of 'roles' they enact.	1.0	1.0	1.0	1.0	2.0	2.0	2.0	2.0

	8. The teacher should be in intimate contact with students and be friendly with them.	a) creates a feeling of love and concern for them by attending individually to their academic and personal problems.	1.0	1.0	1.0	1.0	2.0	2.0	2.0	2.0
		b) doesn't snub or hurt the students by showing their defects, instead encourages helps and shows them the way in which they can overcome their lapses.	1.0	1.0	1.0	1.0	2.0	2.0	2.0	2.0
	9. The teacher should inspire, impress and stimulate students not only by his/her teaching but by his/her personality also.	a) belives and behaves with pleasant manners, habits and approaches.	1.0	1.0	1.0	1.0	3.0	3.0	3.0	3.0
		b) promotes pupils curiosity and interest by clarifying their doubts with appreciation and always speaks good encouraging language.	1.0	1.0	1.0	1.0	2.0	2.0	2.0	2.0

Where C1 = class one

C2 = class two

C3 = Class three

Average gives the consistency of the teacher in expressing the behaviorus in the respective competency.

To avoid unnecessary repetition, of using the word teacher at the beginning of each behaviour in column 3, i.e., behaviours expressed by the teacher, the word 'teacher' has been given at the top of the table.

From the table no. 4.28 for teacher no. 13 it could be found that a total number of nine competencies, and eighteen behaviours expressed in the class room are observed by the researchers. The comparisions made of pre-test and post-test scores and their averages show that for 10 behaviours the average post-test scores are 3.0. It indicates that for 10 behaviours out of 18 behaviours for which the pre-test average scores were mostly 1.0, the teacher had exhibited that particular behaviour. It indicates that the teacher at no. 13 had been empowered to a SUFFICIENT degree.

Table 4.29.—Distribution of pre-test and post-test scores for most essential competencies observed with behaviours expressed by the teacher no. 14 in the class room

Teacher	Competency statements	Behaviours expressed by the teacher	Class room observations of the teacher							
			PRE-TEST				POST-TEST			
			C-1	C-2	C-3	Avg.	C-1	C-2	C-3	Avg.
Teacher No. 14	1. The teacher should maintain discipline in classroom to facilitate smooth instruction.	The teacher a) identifies with the class and never allows monotony to set in by quick shift of presentation.	1.0	1.0	1.0	1.0	2.0	2.0	2.0	2.0
		b) interacts freely with students and at the same time avoids giving excessive freedom by arresting deviated or irrelevant talks and questions of students.	1.0	1.0	1.0	1.0	2.0	2.0	2.0	2.0

(Contd...)

1	2	3	4	5	6	7	8	9	10	11
	2. The teacher should realise the relevance and significance of teaching.	a) utilises all the available opportunities that are beneficial for students viz., field trips, science fares, sports games.	1.0	1.0	1.0	1.0	3.0	3.0	3.0	3.0
		b) teaches all the units of syllabus without fail, if necessary by taking some special classes.	1.0	1.0	1.0	1.0	2.0	2.0	2.0	2.0
	3. The teacher should be honest and sincere.	a) discharges his/her duties with sense like attending to school regularly, taking classes regularly and working for the academic and personality development of his/her pupils.	1.0	1.0	1.0	1.0	2.0	2.0	2.0	2.0
		b) attends to school work entrusted by developing his/her own resources and does it by using best capabilities.	1.0	1.0	1.0	1.0	3.0	3.0	3.0	3.0

	4. The teacher should know the aims, goals and objectives of teaching the subject.	a) makes the children attain the optimum levels of teaching.	0	0	1.0	0.33	3.0	3.0	3.0	3.0
		b) engages students in activities like preparing the charts, clay models and other aids so that the three domains are achieved.	1.0	1.0	1.0	1.0	2.0	2.0	2.0	2.0
	5. The teacher should inspire, impress and stimulate students not only by his/her teaching but by his/her personality also.	a) believes and behaves with pleasant manners, habits and approaches.	0	1.0	1.0	0.66	2.0	2.0	2.0	2.0
		b) promotes pupils curiosity and interest by clarifying their doubts with appreciation and always speaks good encouraging language.	0	0	1.0	0.33	2.0	2.0	3.0	2.3

Where C1 = class one

C2 = class two

C3 = class three

Average gives the consistency of the teacher in expressing the behaviours in the respective competency.

To avoid unnecessary repetition, of using the word teacher at the beginning of each behaviour in column 3, i.e., behaviours expressed by the teacher, the word 'teacher' has been given at the top of the table.

From the table no. 4.29 for teacher no. 14 it could be found that a total number of five competencies, and ten behaviours expressed in the class room are observed by the researchers. The comparisions made of pre-test and post-test scores and their averages indicate that for seven behaviours out of ten the average post-test scores are 2.0 for which the pre-test average scores were mostly 1.0 . It means that for seven behaviours the teacher had exhibited that particular behaviour. It indicates that the teacher at no. 14 had exhibited that particular behaviour. It shows that the teacher at no. 14 had been empowered to a SATISFACTORY degree.

Table 4.30.—Distribution of pre-test and post-test scores for most essential competencies observed with behaviours expressed by the teacher no. 15 in the class room

Teacher	Competency statements	Behaviours expressed by the teacher	Class room observations of the teacher							
			PRE-TEST				POST-TEST			
			C-1	C-2	C-3	Avg.	C-1	C-2	C-3	Avg.
Teacher No. 15	1. The teacher should inculcate moral values in children by giving striking examples from real ilfe situations.	The teacher a) uses simulated situations and reinforces the experted behaviour when exhibited.	0	0	0	0	3.0	3.0	3.0	3.0
		b) organises small role-plays and dramas and makes the children to get the feeling of 'roles' they enact.	0	0	0	0	3.0	3.0	3.0	3.0

(Contd...)

1	2	3	4	5	6	7	8	9	10	11
	2. The teacher should identify the latent talents in children and try to draw out the best in them.	a) encourages pupils to particiate in drawing and painting competitions, elocution, debate, essay writing, science fares and gives them sufficient guidance.	1.0	1.0	1.0	1.0	2.0	2.0	2.0	2.0
		b) maintains an anecdotal record and explores opportunities for his/her pupils.	1.0	1.0	1.0	1.0	2.0	2.0	2.0	2.0
	3. The teacher should inspire, impress and stimulate students not only by his/her teaching but by his/her personality also.	a) belives and behaves with pleasant manners, habits and approaches.								
		b) promotes pupils curiosity and interest by clarifying their doubts with appreciation and always speaks good encouraging language.	0	0	1	0.33	2.0	2.0	2.0	2.0

	4. The teacher should in intimate contact with students and be friendly with them.	a) creates a feeling of love and concern for them by attending individually to their academic and personal problems.	0	0	0	0	2.0	2.0	2.0	2.0
		b) doesn't snub or hurt the students by showing their defects, instead, encourages, helps and shows them the way which they can overcome their lapses.	0	0	0	0	2.0	2.0	2.0	2.0
	5. The teacher should develop easy, original and innovative methods to aid instruction.	a) develops low cost aids by using the material available in school.	1.0	1.0	1.0	1.0	2.0	2.0	2.0	2.0
		b) involves pupils in preparing teaching aids like charts, models to explain concepts relating to mathematics, sciences, languages and arts.	1.0	1.0	1.0	1.0	2.0	2.0	2.0	2.0

(Contd...)

1	2	3	4	5	6	7	8	9	10	11
	6. The teacher must be hard working.	a) corrects the home work of the students by pin-pointing their mistakes.	1.0	1.0	1.0	1.0	3.0	3.0	3.0	3.0
		b) collects more information and material to make his/her lesson interesting and absorbing.	1.0	1.0	1.0	1.0	3.0	3.0	3.0	3.0

Where C1 = class one

C2 = class two

C3 = Class three

Average gives the consistency of the teacher in expressing the behaviours in the respective competency.

To avoid unnecessary repetition, of using the word teacher at the beginning of each behaviour in column 3, i.e., behaviours expressed by the teacher, the word 'teacher' has been given at the top of the table.

From the table no. 4.30 for teacher no. 15 it could be found that a total number of six competencies, and twelve behaviours expressed in the class room are observed by the researchers. The comparisions made of pre-test and post-test scores and their averages show that the average post-test scores for eight behaviurs are 2.0. It means that for eight behavours the teacher had exhibited that particular behaviour. It indictes that the teacher at no. 15 had been empowered to a SATISFACTORY degree from the pre-test average scores for most of the competencies at 1.0.

ANALYSIS AND INFERENCES

From the tables 4.16, to 4.30, it is found that for 15 teachers, competencies and behaviours under the competencies are observed and pre-test and post-test scores are given along with average pre-test and average post-test scores. The observations are made by the researcher while the teachers were attending to their regular classes and discharging thier duties. all the observations have been made by the researchers by making visits to the classes of the 15 teachers while they are on their normal course of work. Prior permission from the principals and the 15 teachers of the three institutes, Andhra Mahila Sabha, Hyderabad, DIET-Neredmet, Hyderabad was taken by the researchers to observe the classes.

For teacher at no. 1- nine competencies, for teacher at no. 2- eight competencies, for eacher at no. 3- ten competencies, for teacher at no. 4- eight competencies, for teacher at no. 5- eight competencies, for teacher at no. 6- eight competencies, for teacher at no. 7- eight competencies, for teacher at no. 8 -seven competencies, for teacher at no. 9- eleven competencies, for teacher at no. 10 -ten competencies, for teacher at no. 11- seven competencies, for teacher at no. 12- eight competencies, for teacher at no. 13 - nine competencies, for teacher at no. 14 - five competencies, for teacher at no. 15 - six competencies along with the behaviours expressed by the teachers in the classroom with pre-test and post-test scores and average pre-test and average post-test scores have been found out. The average pre-test and average post-test scores denotes the consistency of teachers in expressing the behaviour under the respective competencies.

As already explained above, for teacher at no. 14 only five competencies and ten behaviours and for teacher at no. 15 six competencies and twelve behaviours were observed by the researcher. During the pre-test observations made by the researchers for teachers at no.14 and 15 has been found that for teacher at no. 14, for ten competencies average pre-test scores were found to be satisfactory and for teacher at no.15 nine competencies were found to be satisfactory. It shows that the above two teachers had already been empowered in the above said competencies prior to administering the techniques by the researchers. However, the researchers have taken the remaining competencies and post-test observations after administering the techniques were taking for the remaining competencies.

As could be seen from the tables 4.16 to 4.30, a total no.of 122 competencies and 244 behaviurs have been observed for all the 15 teachers. Of the 244 behaviurs, 55 competencies and 110 behaviurs are from Managerial related competencies, 15 competencies and 30 behaviurs are from Curriculum related competencies, 30 competencies and 60 behaviours are from Pupil related competencies and 22 competencies and 44 behaviours are from Value related competencies.

Out of 122 competencies and 244 behaviours observed in the class room for 15 teachers, it is found by the investigator that the maximum number of competencies observed are from Managerial related competencies. The highest number Managerial related competencies observed were for teacher at no. 9 (6 competencies and 12 behaviours). The lowest number was for teachers at no. 14 and 15 which is four.

It is also found that for every teacher atleast three competencies were observed from Managerial related competencies on an average which indicates that those teachers needed maximum empowerment in comeptencies related to Managerial related competency group. It may be said that the teachers had to be empowered in competencies relatd to management and adminsitration of the classroom, motivation of the pupils, development of "self" etc., prior to the administration of techniques. Hence it may be inferred that competencies relating to management and administration of the classroom needed maximum empowerment.

Similarly, from pupil related competencies, a total number of 30 competencies and 60 behaviurs were observed which shows that pupil related competencies needed attention for empowerment for teachers next to Managerial related competencies. In indicates that most of the teachers needed empowerment regariding pupil related competencies like bulding up rapport with students, inspiring and stimulating pupils with their personality and drawing out the latent talents in pupils, etc.

The next group was value related competencies from which it can be found that a total number of 22 competencies and 44 behaviours for observed with an average of atleast one competency for teacher. It is also found that for teachers at no.6, no. 11 and at no. 12 not a single competency was observed from this group. For other teachers it is either one competency or two for every teacher the competency from this group is observed. This indicates that values such as sincerity, honesty, love towards profession and inculcating moral values in children needed empowerment.

lastly from curriculum related competency group the competencies observed were only 15 in all and 30 behaivours. For five teachers (teachers at nos. 2, 4,5,13,15) no competency was observed by the researchers and for five teachers one competency was observed and for five teachers two competencies were observed. It may indicate that out of 15 teachers only 5 teachers needed maximum empowerment int he competencies related to this group.

After careful observation of the data in the tables from 4.16 to 4.30 for 15 teachers and their competencies and behaviorus, the competencies which occurred frequently from the four grouops which needed empowerment in the order of preference are given in the follwoing pages separately from mangerial related, value related, pupil related and curriculum related competencies. Under Managerial related competency grouop the competency which occurred most number of times (11 times) is "The teacher should develop easy, orignial and innovative methods to aid instruction", which indicates that most of the teachers needed sufficient guidance in developing innovative methods for pupils to teach. The next competency which needed empowerment is "the teacher should maintain discipline in classroom to facilitate smooth instruction", which indicates that most teachers needed empowerment regarding discipline in the classroom. Similarly the other two competencies which needed empowerment are "The teacher should be resourceful person" and "The teacher should be hard working".

In the same manner from value related competency group the most frequently occurred competency was "The teacher should develop moral values in children by giving striking examples from real life situations, and secondly "The teacher should be honest and sincere" which needed emphasis regarding empowerment in the order of preference in teachers.

From pupil related competency group, the most frequently occurred competencies wre "The teacher should inspire, impress and stimulate students not only by teaching but by his personality also", and "the teacher should identify the latent talents in students and try to draw out the best in them", which needed empowerment in the order of preference in teachers.

Lastly, from curriculum related competency group the competency "The teacher should know the aims, goals and objectives of teaching the subject" was the one which needed maximum priority to be empowered in the teachers.

The researchers have analysed the data of all the 15 teachers and inferences are drawn by analysing all the 15 teachers competencies. Since the purpose of the study is to find out whether empowerment is possible in teachers after undergoing training for a period of time, the inferences taken from the 15 teachers gives a more useful information rather than the information obtained after analysing the teacher separately.

From the tables, it is evident that competencies under managerial related competency group are highest in number. It means that a majority of teachers have given highest preference to competencies regaridng class-room administration skills of professional and personal development, administrative skills. The pre-test scores also suggest that most of the teachers are deficient in managerial related competencies and needed considerable empowerment of these competencies.

In the second place competencies from pupil related competency group denotes that teachers gave importance to the competencies which facilitates pupils learning and which are useful for the pupils.

In the third place value related competencies denote that values like honesty, sincerity and love towards profession are felt necessary by the teachers.

In the last place curriculum related competencies denote that most of the teachers have sufficient knowledge regarding the content and methodology of subjects they teach.

FINAL OUTCOME OF THE RESEARCH

After careful observation and comparisions made by the researchers between pre-test and post-test scores and also the averages of all the 15 teachers, the following observations have been made by the researchers regarding the empowerment of teachers. The outcome of the research for 15 teachers has been given in the following pages.

Out of 15 teackers taken as a sample by the researchers for empowerment, eight teachers had been empowered to a 'satisfactory' degree. The average post-test score of 2.0 also indicates that there had been 'satisfactory' raise in their competency base. The teachers who have been empowered to a satisfactory degree are Teacher at no.1 (table 4.16) teacher at no.3 (table 4.18), teacher at no. 11 (table 4.26) teacher at no. 13 (table 4.28)) teacher at no.14 (table no.4.29) and teacher at no.15 (table 4.30).

For teacher at no.1, teacher at no.3, teacher at no.6, teacher at no.10, teacher at no. 11 it has been observed that the average pre-test score which is either '0' or less than '1' the post-test average score has been raised to '2' for most of the behaviours. It indicates that eachers, thoguh initially not exhibiting the behavour in the classroom could incorporate the techniques in their teaching and exhibit the behaviours twice in each class and thus 'satisfactorily' been empowered.

Teachers at no. 14 and teacher at no.15 had average pre-test scores of 1.0 for most of the behaviours observed by the researchers in the classroom. As already mentioned earlier in this chapter only five competencies and ten behaviours were observed for teacher at no.14 and six competencies and twelve behaivours were observed for the teacher at no.15. The teacher had been empowered to a 'satisfactory' level which is indicated by the average post-test scores of '2.0' for most of the behaviorus of the two teachers. Similarly six teachers i.e. teacher at no.2 (table no. 4.17) teacher at no.4 (table no. 4.19), teacher at no.5 (table no. 4.20), teacher at no.7 (table no. 4.22), teacher at no.8 (table 4.23) and teacher at no. 12 (table 4.27) have been empowered to a 'sufficient' degree, though for most of the teachers the average pre-test scores were mostly '0' which means that the respective behaviours were not exhibited by them in the class prior to the techniques administered byt he researchers. It may be said that these teachers could utilise the techniques to a maximum extent and thus have been empowered to a 'sufficient' level.

In the case of teacher at no.9 (table no. 4.24) the average pre-test scores as well as average post-test scores are not at all encouraging. The teacher could not empower any of his competencies either to a 'satisfactory' level or to a 'sufficient' level which is indicated by the average post-test scores of 1.0 or less than 1.0 for all the elven competencies and twenty behaviours observed by the researchers. So, it is felt by the researchers that the teacher at no.9 may not fit into the teaching profession and may be entrusted with other tasks related to management, administration and allied fields which are other than teacing. However, ti is only a personal view of the researchers which have its limitations.

With the above analysis and inference it has been found that out of fifteen teachers fourteen teachers could empower their competencies either to 'satisfactory' or 'sufficient' level. **Hence the hypothesis no.3 which is formulated as "It is possible to inculcate the desirable characteristics in teachers and empower them to become better in profession" proved to be tenable and hence retained.**

FURTHER SUGGESTIONS FOR NURTURING THE COMPETENCIES IN TEACHERS

During the discussions and interactions held while conducting seminar, symposium, discussion and other techniques with the teacher educators (trainees), many suggestions had emerged for nurturing the characteristics that are taken up as useful for empowering a teacher. They are consolidated and presented in the following paragraphs for facilitating the growth and development of the competencies in teachers. They are inaddition to the specific training activities presented earlier in this chapter. These are as follows.

1. The following points are some practical suggestions useful for the teacher in organising the classroom effieciently and maintianing discipline inc lassroom (competency no.4 in table 4.15).

1. **Maintain dignity:** The teacher should not lower his/her dignity by getting involved in unseemly arugments with children, teacher should be a good example fo what he/she could like the chikdren to admire. Avoid trying to be popular with the children.

2. **Be consistent:** The teacher should not be strict with discipline one day and slack another. The teacher should not show favoritism to any pupil, and shouldn't

allow his/her empotions to control his/her actions. The teacher shouldn't take action over a child when the temper is lost; should wait till it is regained. A sympathetic and understanding attitude to children is not a sign of weakness but of strength.

3. **Avoid monotony :** When the teacher feels the children are not interested in a particular topic of a lesson, the teacher should quickly shift the presentation and after regaining the interst at the pupils, should continue the lesson. In this gap the teacher may engage pupils by telling some stories, giving them some constructive work etc. activities.

4. **Use punishment and Rewards wisely :** Never allow punishments to become a form of revenge. Child can become hardened to punishment too frequentlyg iven, make the punishment appropriate not only to the offense but to the offender also.

The following disorders are representative of the kind of trouble the teacher has to deal with in class.

1. Inattention and Restlessness caused by

a. Attractions or distrubances outside the classroom.

b. Excess energy accumulated by children kept passive and inactive for too long.

c. Children who are physically or mentally tired.

d. Lessons which are boring.

2. Noise arising from

a. Over-eager children with bad manners who snap their fingers and call out "I Sir!" when they know the answer to a question or wish to be chosen for some activity.

b. Private or group arguments which lead to quarrelling.

c. Whispers and subdued laughter.

3. Deliberate naughtiness

This can take a great many forms such as rudeness, disobedience, lying, stealing etc. The actual cause may le deeply bureid in the child's subconscious, ir it may be a superficial expression of the independence that growing children like to assert. So, it is always better to find the root cause, for rebellion is ultimately a spiritual problem and treatment must be with full understanding, if it is to be effective.

How to prevent disorder in the class room?

1. Ensure there is enough work to keep every child occupied.
2. Check to see that every child knows what he is supposed to do.
3. Keep an eye on the problem children to prevent work breakdown.
4. Achieve a working harmony between pupils and the teacher.

3. For empowering competency no.6 (the teacher should be hardowrking) while correcting the errors in the note books of the pupils, the teacher can keep in mind the following symbols for making the note book work.

Under a misspelling	———
Under a bad mispelling	═══
To indicate letter (s) or word (s) missed out	⋌
To separate two words that have been written as one	/
A new paragraph required	‖
To indicate the need for joining words	⁀ ‿
To indicate that a comment has been written in the margin	*

4. For empowering competency no. 13, (The teacher should identify latent talents in students and try to draw out the best in them) table no. 4.15 the researchers tried to empower the skill of probing questions through "Micro-teaching" for teachers to know the latent talents in students.

To make pupils think and discover facts teachers have to master the art of questioning. Pupils respond in a number of ways and styles such as no response, wrong response, partially correct response, incomplete response or correct response depending upon their own development level, nature of questions and teacher's behaviour.

The skill of probing questions consists of the following techniques.

1. Prompting
2. Seeking further information
3. Refocusing
4. Redirectiion and
5. Increasing critical awareness

(i) **Prompting :** It refers to the cues or hints provided by the teacher through well framed questions to a pupil for arriving at the desired response, incorrect, partially correct or incomplete responses. Using this the teacher can prompt students to know their innate talents.

(ii) **Seeking further information :** This is a technique of getting additional information from the responding pupil to bring his initial incomplete or partially correct response to the desired response level. The questions like, "What else can you say? How can you make it more clear? Can you give some examples/evidences etc. are often used for seeking further information from pupils.

(iii) **Refocusing :** This technique is used in a correct response situation to strengthen the response given by the pupil. The teacher persuades the responding pupil either to relate his response with something already studied by him or to consider implications of his response in more complex and noble situations. The questions like, How does it differ from ... similar to ...? Can you give an example to support your answer? etc. are involved in refocusing.

(iv) **Redirection :** This technique is generally applied in a 'no response' 'incomplete response' situation. It requires putting or edirecting the same question to several pupils for eliciting desired response.

(v) **Increasing critical awareness :** A teacher is required to ask 'how' and 'why' of a completely correct or desired response from the responding pupil. The questions like, 'How can you justify it? Why do you answer so? How does it occur? etc. increase the critical awareness.

The Teacher Behaviour Observation Schedule (TBOS) for probing questions is as follows:

Time interval (each 30 seconds)

1 2 ..... 11, 12

1. Prompting (P)
2. Seeking further information (SFI)
3. Refousing (RF)
4. Redirection (RD)
5. Increasing Critical Awareness (CA)

(5) For empoering instruction management and lesson planning skill, the following suggestions are made for empowering the above competency. (Table no. 4.15)

Developing communication skill is achieved in the following manner. However, perfect communication is almost impossible to achieve because it depends on so many variables. For success, the process demands that the 'message' be put into a suitable 'code', such as language or gesture, and be transmitted by the 'sender' to the 'receiver' using appropriate medium such as correspondence, broadcasting etc. However, the message must contend with interference from what technically is called 'noise'. This is made up of physical interference such as distance or extraneous noise, by 'mental interference' caused either by the receiver not knowing the code or being distracted from attending to the message, or by 'emotional interference', as when there is a bad personal relationship between the sender the receiver.

Verbal communication with its need for careful sequencing of ideas and a choice of vocabularly that is well within the capacity of children should be of utmost consideration.

Nonverbal communication is an important means of sending messages between people. A simple gesture such as a smile can tell someone else a great deal about how you feel towards them. A slight movement of the land can beckon some one to you and a handshake can indicate more truthfully than the words.

For good communication, the following points are to be considered.

(a) The message (the teaching point one wants to get access to get across to pupils).

* How clear is it in you mind?

* How does it need to be shaped to make it as clear to the receiver as it is to you?

(b) The receiver (each one of pupils)

* What codes does he know?

* What knowledge does he have that will enable him to make sense of the message.

(c) The code (verbal, non verbal)

* What codes are available to you that the receiver know?

* which of these is the most efficient for this occasion.

(d) The medium (audio visual aids, chalk and talk, pictures, models)

* What media are available in school?
* Which will be most appropriate for the message?

(e) The noise (in attention, lack of interest, knowledge or limited experience)

What possible forms of noise will your (teacher) message have to compete with?

* How can some of these form of noise be removed or reduced?

To empower the lesson planning skill a model example of information lesson is given below for the use of the teacher.

Although many lessons will contain a variety of features such as information, practice, appreciation etc. the information lesson is the commonest type. It is essentially a lesson in which new knowedge is gained. Some suggestions in which an information lesson can be developed is given as under.

1. Introduction

One or more of the following methods may be used.

(a) *Questioning :* This may be to stimulate the previous knowledge which are relevant to the lesson. Question should be carefully taught by the teacher beforehand.

(b) *Visual aids and Demonstration :* Demonstration with visual aids has great value in concertrating the attention of children. In mathematics aids like cylinder, cone, cube etc. give a real and 3-dimensional view for the children and facilitate better learning.

(c) *Activity :* It is useful in subjects like mathematics and language where rigorous mental activity in the form of making the children recited a poem in language or recollect the principles and formula's in mathematics.

(d) *Mystery :* If an object to be in the lesson is brought into the class concealed in the teacher' pocket, which is obviours and due to the bulge noticable, the curoisity of the children will be immediately aroused. Such an introduction raises the children's appetite for learning and is a useful introduction if used occasionally.

2. Presentation : The presentation should be a record of the facts to be taught and methods to be used to make this relationship clear in the lesson notes, the content should be written under headings or steps so that the teacher can know at a glance what the next step is, which teaching aids should be kept ready for the lesson. Teaching skills such as questioning, story telling, discussion, drawing, modeling and dramatization can also be used.

3. Conclusion : Some teachers regard the main pupil's activity has the conclusion of an information lesson. Others like to have the last moments to draw the threads of the lesson together, recapitualating the main points or giving pointer as to what will follow in the next lesson on the subject.

5

SUMMARY AND CONCLUSIONS

A bird's eye-view of the entire study pertaining to the topic "Empowering Primary Teachers with Necessary Competencies is provided in the succeeding paragraphs.

SUMMARY AND CONCLUSIONS

The total study has been divided into five chapters including the present one.

The first chapter, INTRODUCTION, describes the need of a teacher to become a competent individual and the researcher tries to present supportive material for teacher empowerment. The researchers also introduce the reader to the present problem after giving information regarding teacher empowerment. Any educational system cannot last long, if its pillars are not deeply rooted. The teachers have to perform multiple tasks as a guru, friend, social worker, responsible citizen, philosopher and a seeker of truth to see that the pillars are laid strong. A competent teacher can induce responsibility, sincerity, moral values, positive attitudes in children and can also influence the education system. Unless the teacher is competent, the educational system cannot become perfect. Competency go hand in hand with responsibility. So, if the teacher is competent and feels 'responsibility', he can discharge his duties well.

It is always desirable and essential rather, that a teacher should intrinsically motivated and competent enough in the skills necessary to perform his duties well, so that he can motivate the pupils to learn since a teacher is the one who opens the eyes (minds) if pupils to the world of knowledge, first, he should be an enlightened individual. Hence, proper 'enlightenment' should be given to a teacher and the essential competencies are to be empowered. A competent teacher is a precious gift for the pupils as well as the society also. Unless the teacher is competent, and possess some skills to discharge his duties perfectly, he can't induce the same qualities in children. So, he must be competent enough to discharge his duties as a teacher, friend, guide, philosopher and an advanced traveller in the path of knowledge and mould the personality of his pupils.

The second chapter, 'DETAILS OF THE PROBLEM,' explains the statement of the problem, operational definitions, objectives of the study, review of related literature, hypotheses and limitations of the study.

The main objectives of the study are:

1. To identify the necessary competencies to be possessed by teachers in general at primary level of education.

2. To identify the most essential competencies in teachers at primary level of education.

3. To develop the means and measures to inculcate and nurture the most essential competencies in teachers at primary level of education.

To realise the above objectives the researcher has formulated the following hypotheses respectively for first, second and third objectives.

The Hypotheses of the study are :

1. A few competencies are necessary to be possessed by teachers as viewed commonly by Teacher Educators, Primary Teachers and also by the Teachers Trainees.

2. Some most essential characteristics competencies do exist in teachers which are to be considered as an essential requirement for teachers entering teaching profession at primary level of education.

3. It is possible to inculcate the most essential competencies in teachers and empower them to become better teachers.

The review of literature explains some of the work done regarding teacher competencies and characteristics some of which are. Hart revealed size most frequently mentioned characteristics as of the teacher has teaching skills, cheerful, and compassionate, interested in pupils, impartial fair. THE CBTE movement defined five types of competencies cognitive based, performance based, consequence based, affective and exploratory and gave a detailed explanation of the competencies. Avalos, Lockhood and Vespoor found that the general knowledge base of elementary teachers in acknowledged to impact negatively in various ways of performance.

The third chapter 'RESEARCH AND DESIGN', includes area covered by the researcher, selection, of sample, development of opinionnaire, pilot study, mailing the opinonnaire for experts opinion, final form of the opinionnare, administration of the opinionnaire.

The researchers covered all the districts in Andhra Pradesh. The sample taken for the study comprises teacher educators, primary teachers and teacher trainees. An opinionnaire was developed by taking the characteristics and competencies found from review of literature and books in form of statements to establish validity and comprehensibility, the raw opinionnaire was sent to experts. The items were deleted which the experts opined to be inessential for the study. Then the final opinionnaire with 50 statements is prepared and mailed to the sample. The researchers received 93 opinionnaires from teacher eductors, 183 from primary teachers and 92 from teacher trainees. The primary teachers who work in Govt. and Zilla Parished schools, DIET lectures and lecturers and lecturers of colleges of education and prospective teachers or teachers trainees who have completed their B.Ed. and pursuing their M. Ed. are also taken as sample. The respondents were asked to put a tick mark (3) against the alternatives most essential, essential and least essential for each competency statement. Thus the data from a total number of 368 persons comprising teacher educators, primary teachers and teacher trainees was collected. The analysis and inferences are explained in the fourth chapter.

The fourth chapter 'ANALYSIS AND INFERENCES' discusses the way data was analysed and inferences were drawn. The fifty competencies were grouped into six heads - Managerial related competencies, School related competencies, Value related competencies, Community related competencies, Pupil related competencies and Curriculum related competencies. This was done adhering to the opinions expressed by experts and all the 50 competencies arranged into six groups.

Then the actual frequencies were converted into percentages to give a clearer picture to the reader regarding the respondents who opted for most essential, essential and least essential characteristics.

These percentages were then used to perform chi-square test and carrying out he statistical analysis further. Then chi-square test was carried out to know whether equal probability hypothesis was tenable or not. It revealed if the differences found in respondents' option of the three alternatives most essential, essential and least essential was real or due to chance factor or real. Thus the researchers carried out chi-square test for each competency for teacher eductors, primary teachers and teacher trainees separately. The chi-square values were them compared with the table value at df(2) and the competencies which were not found significant at 0.05 and 0.01 levels have been deleted for consideration. Thus competencies nos. 5, 26, 33 were deleted for consideration since they were not found to be significant at 0.01 or at 0.05 level.

To find out the most essential characteristics the highest percentage of preferences given by teacher educators, primary teachers and teacher trainees was taken under the alternative 'Most Essential'. A minimum percentage of 50 was taken as a cut off score. This information yielded the most essential characteristics desired by teacher educators, primary teachers and teacher trainees commonly. Similarly 'essential' competencies were also found out taking 50 per cent as cut off score under 'essential' alternative again opted by all the three types of respondents commonly. Thus the researchers established 15 Most Essential competencies and 12 essential competencies commonly preferred by teacher educators, primary teachers and teacher trainees. The 15 most essential competencies that are established by the researchers have been given as under.

1. The teacher should realise the relevance and significance of teaching.
2. The teacher should be ever ready to learn new things and constantly augment his knowledge base.
3. The teacher should motivate pupils and incite interest in them to learn.
4. The teacher should maintain discipline in classroom to facilitate smooth instruction.
5. The teacher should be a resourceful person.
6. The teacher should be hard working.
7. The teacher should develop easy, original and innovative methods to aid instruction.
8. The teacher should be honest and sincere.
9. The teacher should love his profession.
10. The teacher should develop moral values in children by giving striking examples from real life situations.
11. The teacher should be in intimate contact with students and be friendly with them.
12. The teacher should stimulate, impress, and inspire students not only by his teaching but by his personality also.

13. The teacher should identify the latent talents in students and try to draw out the best in them.
14. The teacher should know the aims, goals and objectives of teaching the subject.
15. The teacher should plan his lesson well and know the skills of instructional management.

Similarly, the 12 essential competencies have also been established by the researchers which are given as under.

1. The teacher should evaluate students' performance from time to time and give appropriate work for the gifted and remedial work for the substandard.
2. The teacher should attend to various teacher training programmes and improve his/her teaching competency.
3. The teacher should be cheerful and active.
4. The teacher should communicate the pupils' progress in various areas—cognitive, affective and psychomotor to parents by conducting meetings with them regularly.
5. The teacher should be aware of our cultural heritage and pass it on to students.
6. The teacher must have consistent pattern in action and policy.
7. The teacher must seek co-operation from the society and self-government institutions and ensure their participation to improve the quality of education.
8. The teacher should keep in view the individual differences of intellect in students and adopt suitable teaching techniques.
9. The teacher should encourage activity based learning among students.
10. The teacher should possess guidance and counseling skills to organize, guidance and counseling sessions for the needy and maladjusted students.

11. The teacher must be sympathetic and understanding in finding a solution to pupils' personal and academic problems.

12. The teacher should effectively related the subject matter in one area to other areas of the curriculum.

Thus the fifteen most essential competencies and twelve essential competencies were found out by the researchers and they were considered as NECESSARY competencies. The above twelve essential competencies should be considered as desirable competencies for the teachers entering teaching profession at primary level. But the fifteen most essential competencies should be considered as highly required competencies without which the teacher will become incompetent to teach.

For the 15 most essential competencies, techniques to empower the same in teachers were suggested by the researchers. The techniques were administered for the teachers and the extent to which empowerment was done was verified by the researchers by making class room observations. The techniques administered to empower teachers were 1. role-play, 2. modeling, 3. observation, 4. micro-teaching 5. seminar, discussion and symposium and 6. brain-storming.

The techniques were administered to 15 teachers who were working as Secondary Grade Assistants and having three years of teaching experience in Mandal Parishad elementary schools. They were taking in-service training in various Colleges of Education in Krishna District, A.P. Teachers with different methodologies like Mathematics, Biological and Physical Sciences, English, Social studies were taken.

Before administering the techniques for empowerment of teachers, the researchers have observed them by personally observing their classes in institutions while they were engaged in teaching. This was done to know if the teachers had possessed any of the 15 most essential characteristics which make them competent to teach. Since it is difficult to measure all the competencies directly, the researchers have developed two behaviours for each competency as the criteria to measure the degree with which the competencies were present in the teachers. Thus for 15 competencies a total number of 30 behaviours were developed. A maximum of 3 classes were observed by the researchers for the 15 teachers and the pre-test scores were taken down only for those competencies which were not found in the teachers (i.,e., the teachers who could not express the behaviours in the class room). The following scoring procedure has been adopted by the researchers for the pre-test scores.

For every competency if a particular behaviour is expressed by the teacher in the class room 3 or more times, a score of 3 was given. If the behaviour was expressed two time a score of 2 was awarded. Similarly if it was expressed only one time, a score of 1 and if was not expressed at all even once, a score of 0 was awarded. Along with this motivation of the pupils in the class room was also observed and scores were given accordingly. Thus pre-test scores were taken by the researchers for all the 15 teachers for the competencies and behaviours whose scores were 0 and 1.

Later for 15 teachers training was given using the techniques mentioned above and means and ways of empowering the 15 competencies were also suggested by the researchers. After completion of the administration a gap of 1 month was given during which period the teachers were requested to incorporate the means and ways in their teaching and thus empower themselves to become better in their profession. The researchers have again taken the post-test scores for the 15 teachers by observing their classes to know the effect and impact of the training given for the teachers earlier.

The researchers found out that out of 15 teachers taken for study and given training, 14 teachers had been empowered. Of these 15 teachers 8 teachers had been empowered to a 'satisfactory' degree. Six teachers had been empowered to a 'sufficient' degree. Only one teacher had not been empowered. From this it was concluded by the researchers that the techniques administered for the teachers were found useful for them to empower their competencies.

Thus the first objective, 'to identify the necessary competencies to be possessed by teachers in general at primary level of education' as tested through Hypothesis no : 1 "A few competencies are necessary to be possessed by teachers as viewed commonly by teacher educators, primary teachers and also by teachers trainees" has been realised as described and discussed in Chapter IV.

The second objective "to identify the most essential competencies in teachers at primary level" as tested through Hypothesis No : 2. 'Some most essential competencies do exist in teachers which are to be considered as an essential requirement for teachers entering teaching profession level of education' has been realised as discussed in Chapter IV.

The third objective "To develop the means and measures to inculcate and nurture the identified competencies in teachers" is tested through Hypotheis no : 3, i.e., "It is possible to inculcate the most essential competencies in individuals and empower them to become better teachers" has been realised as described and discussed in Chapter IV.

Thus the study concludes that

1. A few competencies are necessary to be possessed by teachers as viewed commonly by teachers educators, primary teachers and also by teacher trainees.
2. Some most essential competencies do exist in teachers which are to be considered as an essential requirement for teachers entering teaching profession at primary level of education.
3. It is possible to inculcate the most essential competencies in individuals and empower them to become better teachers.

IMPLICATIONS OF THE STUDY

1. This study made to empower teachers with necessary competencies is only an attempt made by the researchers to throw some light on the various competencies which

a competent teacher should possess. As it is difficult and rather impractical to measure values like honesty, sincerity, love, hard working, etc., a set of behavioural traits has been adopted to describe the most essential competencies which enable the teacher to become competent in the profession. Therefore these behavioural traits, though not exhaustive, will be of immense help for quantifying certain abstract qualities in teacher.

2. Like wise, the activities planned to empower competencies and the means and ways described in this report have been developed mostly from the ideas and teaching experience of the investigators as a teacher and as a teacher educator. So, these activities are only illustrative and are not exhaustive. The teachers may develop some more fitting means to accord their local environment and can modify them to suit the needs of their pupils. The activities given by the researchers will be of some help to the creative teachers who are enthusiastic and enjoy teaching.

3. The most essential competencies and the essential competencies which have been found out by the researchers are not exhaustive. In future, many more competencies may be required for a teacher as the role of teacher has been under tremendous change with the ever changing educational technology and especially with computer education completely influencing every field. Education field is not an exception to this. Naturally, the role of educator also changes accordingly. Hence a number of other competencies may be required for a teacher to become competent in future along with the necessary competencies found out by the researcher.

4. The essential competencies which are suggested by the researchers have been found out with a view that during the recruitment of teachers for primary level, these competencies can be considered as desirable and may be incorporated in entrance examination to attract

competent teachers into teaching profession. So the researchers feel that there should be proper method of recruiting teachers through which the teaching aptitude of the individual is tested thoroughly and is given utmost importance. For this some questions may be developed by the authorities during the entrance examination for recruitment of teachers at District and State Levels, keeping in view the necessary competencies found out by the researchers. The necessary competencies found out by the researchers may be of some help in this regard.

5. It is desired by the researchers that the teachers who had been empowered through the techniques along with the means and ways of empowering them will incorporate them in their teaching and become better teachers. They can in turn make their pupils also highly motivated and thus make learning meaningful and joyful experience to pupils.

SUGGESTIONS FOR FURTHER WORK

1. This being a study based on the attitudes and opinions of the teachers, the outcome of the research may not give hundred per cent information regarding the competencies. Research in social sciences is always susceptible to further developments and modifications. Moreover, the study though extended to a period of four years may not be sufficient to give complete information. Hence, an exhaustive study may be taken up by some National Educational Agency and Competency Based Teaching should be given maximum priority in teaching. In this direction agencies like NCERT, NCTE, NIEPA, UGC can come forward to develop essential competencies in teachers from time to time.

2. The outcome of the activities may be assessed in real life situations after organizing the activities. These kind of activities should be multiplied from time to time by

developing some more techniques in addition to brainstorming, micro-teaching, symposium, seminar, modeling, etc.

3. Research can be carried out on teachers at secondary and higher level and more comprehensive study with a larger sample can be taken up.

BIBLIOGRAPHY

Anand, K.K. (1961). "Selection of men school teachers". Ph.D. Psychology, Punjab University.

Arora (1978). "Differences between effective and ineffecive teachers" New Delhi: S Chand n Company Ltd., 111-130.

Asthana, A.S. (1986)."(Teaching competence: As a state of being and quality". Perspectives in Education 2 No.1

Avalos, B. (1991). "Approaches to Teacher Education." Initial Teacher Training, Commonwealth Secretariat, London.

Avalos, Lockheed and Verspoor (1988). "Primary teachers and Policy Innovation in India". As found in Teacher Education in India edited by Dr. D. Bhaskara Rao. Discvoery publishing house. New Delhi.

Bailkeri, K.N. (1983). "Effect of self-Instructional Remedial Micro Teaching Course on the instructional competence of Inservice Secondary School Maths Teachers". Ph.D. Edn. As found in fourth survey of Research in Education 1984-89. NCERT -New Delhi.

Bandura, A. and Walters, R.H. (1963). "Social learning and Personality Development". Newyork: Holt, Rinehart and Winston.

Bandur, A. and Mc. Donald, F.J. (1963). "The Influence of social Reinforcement and the Behaviour of Models in shaping children's Moral Judgements". Journal of Abnormal and Social Psychology.

Bandura, A (1971). "Vicarious and self-reinforcement processes". In R. Glaser (ed). The Nature of Reinforcement. Columbus: Merrill.

Bandura, A. (1969). "Social-learning Theory of Identificatory Processes". In D.A. Goslin (ed), Handbook of socialisation Theory and Research. Chicago: Rand Mcally, 213-262.

Bhagoliwal, S. (1982). "A study of personality characteristics Associated with Teaching Effectiveness as seen through Rorschach Technique". Ph.D. Edn., A.U.

Bhaskara Rao, D. (1997) . "Success Story of a Primary Education Project". New Delhi: APH Publishing corporation.

Bhaskara Rao, D. and Sambasiva Rao, K.R.S. (1966) "Current Trends in Indian Education", New Delhi : Discovery Publishing House.

Bhaskara Rao, Digumarti, ed (1996). "Encyclopaedia of Education For All". 5 Volumes. New Delhi APH Publishing Corporation.

Bhaskra Rao, Digumarti, ed (2001). "International Encyclopaedia of Science and Technology Education", 11 Volumes.

Bhaskara Rao, Digumarti, ed (2001). "International Encyclopaedia of Human Rights", 7 volumes, New Delhi: Discovery Publshing House.

Bhaskara Rao, Digumarti, ed. (2000). "International Encyclopaedia of AIDS, 11 volumes New Delhi : Discovery Publishing House.

Bhaskara Rao, Digumarti and Digumarti Pushpa Latha, eds. (1998). "International Encyclopaedia of Women", 5 volumes New Delhi : Discovery Publishing House.

Bhattacharjee, R. (1981). "Effectiveness of Micro Teaching in Developing teaching competence", External Service Dept., Shillong. As found in Buch Third surey of Research in Education. 1978-83. NCERT-New Delhi.

Blake, R.R. (1958). "The other person in the situation" In R. Tagiuri and L. Petrullo (eds), Person Perception and Interpersonal Behaviur Stanford, California: Stanford University Press, pp. 229-242

Boyce, A.C. (1912). "Qualities of merit in secondary school teachers". Journal of Educational psychology vol. 3: 144-157.

Brokkover. W.B. (1935). "The relation of social factors to teaching ability". Journal of Experimental Education 13: pp. 191-205.

Buch, M.D (1986). "Third Survey of Research in Education"- 1978-83 NCERT. p. 750.

Burke, A. (1997). "Professionalisation and Teacher Empowerment". DPEP calling. volume. 15. M.H.R.D. New Delhi.

California University (1979). "A study conducted on teacher characteristics". Dept. of Psychology. University of California. U.S.A.

Campbell, D.T. (1961). "Conformity in psychology theories of acquired Behavioural Dispositions". In I.A.Berb and B.M. Bass (eds), Conformity and Deviation. Newyork: Harper p.p. 101-114.

Carlile, A.F. and Fuller (1954). "Predicting performance in the teaching profession". Journal of Educational research 47. p.p. 641-48.

Charter and Waples (1929). "Competency Based Teaching". AS found in International Encyclopaedia of Education, Research and studies. Edited by Torsten Husen and Postlethwaite, T.N., Pergamon Press. vol.2. 1988.

Chathley, Y.P. (1984). "An experimental study of the teaching competency at macro level as a function of training in micro skills among the prospective secondary school teachers in relation to the integration of skills and subject area". Ph.d.edn. Pan. U. As found in Buch Fourth survey of Research in Education. 1984-89. NCERT- New Delhi.

CBTE (1972) "International Encyclopedia of Education, Research and studies. Competency Based Teaching". Edited by Torsten Husen and Postlethwaite, T.N. Pergamon Press, vol.2. 1988.

Coleman, J. *et.al.* (1966) "Equality of Educational opportunity". Washington D.C. : U.S. Government printing office.

Dewey, J (1929). "Sources of Science of Education". Newyork : Liveright, p.p. 13-14.

Digumarti, Bhaskara Rao, ed. (1996). "National Policy on Education" 2 volumes New Delhi : Anmol Publications. **Digumarti, Bhaskara Rao, ed (1998).** National Policy on Education : Towards an Human and Enlightened Society". New Delhi: Discovery Publishing House.

Dutt, B.S.V., Bhaskara Rao, D. and Swamy, C. V.P. (1997). "Self Evaluation in Student Teaching". New Delhi: Discovery Publishing House. p.1

Ediger, Marlow (1998). "Competency Based Teacher Education: help or Hindrance?" In *D. Bhaskara Rao* (ed.), Teacher Education in India, New Delhi: Discovery Publishing House. p.p. 264-267.

Ediger, Marlow and D. Bhaskara Rao (1996). "Science Curriculum". New Delhi : Discovery Publishing House. **Ediger, Marlow and d. Bhaskara Rao (2000).** "Teaching Mathematics Successfully". New Delhi. Discovery Publishing House.

Ediger, Marlow and D. Bhaskara Rao (2000). "Teaching Reading Successfully" New Delhi : Discovery Publishing House.

Ediger, Marlow and D. Bhaskara Rao (2001) "Teaching Science Successfully". New Delhi : Discovery Publishing House.

Ediger, Marlow and D. Bhaskara Rao (2001). "Teaching Social Studies Successfully". New Delhi : Discovery Publishing House.

Eliassen, R.H. and Martin, R.L. (1940). "Pre-training selection of teacher. Educational admn. and supervision" vol. 26 : p.p. 481-92.

Flanders, J.P. (1968). "A Review of research on Imitative behaviour" Psychological bulletin . p.p. 316-337.

Furst, N. and Hill, R.A. (1971). "Systematic classroom observation". The Encyclopedia of Education. Chief Editor for Lee. C. Deighton. U.S. The Macmillan and freepress. vol.9.

Gangappa, M.A. (1969). "Mental Health of a teacher". Educational India. vol. 35. p.p. 263-66.

Guilford. (1956). "Fundamental statistics in psychology and Education". Newyork: Mc graw-hill Book Company.

Hallak, J. (1990). "Investing in the Future." Setting Educational Priorities in the Developing World. IIEP- UNESCO, Paris.

Hargreaves (1994). As found in Primary teachers policy innovation in India. C. Dyer. DPEP calling. vol. 15. New Delhi.

Hart (1936). International Encyclopedia of Education, Research and Studies. Competency Based Teaching. Edited by Torsten Husen and Postlethwaite, T.N. Pergamon Press. vol. 2. 1988.

Heil, *et.al.* (1960). "Characteristics of teachers behaviour and competency related to the achievement of different kinds of children in several elementary grades". Newyork: Office of testing and research Brooklyn College.

Heneveld, W; Craig, H. (1995). "Effective Schools." Determining which factors have the greatest impact". In DAE Newsletter, vol. 7, No. 3, Paris, July-September.

International Commission on Education for 21st Century (1996). Report to UNESCO. Paris. p. 144.

Jayamma, M.S. (1962). "Construction and standardisation of an inventory for predicting teacher efficiency" (for primary school teachers of Mysore state) Ph.D. Edn. Mysore University.

Jhon, E.R., Chesler, P., Bartlett, F. and Victor, I. (1968). "Observation Learning in Cats". Science, 159: 1489-91.

Joyce (1980). "International Encyclopedia of Education and Technology". Modeling in Micro-teaching in G.R. Maclead. and Michael Grant Edition 1989.

Kaur, B. (1983). "An investigation into dimension of teacher effectiveness as perceived by secondary school college and university students". Ph.D. Edn. H.P.U. As found in M.D. Buch. Third survey of Research in Education. 1979-83. NCERT-New Delhi.

Khajuria, D.P. (1981). "The typical patterns of classroom verbal behaviour exhibited to successful teachers of language and science at secondary level". Ph.D. Edn. Jammu U. as found in M.D. Buch. Third survey of Research in Education. 1979-83. NCERT-New Delhi.

Knox, W.B. (1957). "Situational factors in teacher placement and success". Journal of Experiemental Education. 20 p.p. 1-77.

Kothari (1970). "Education and National Development". Report of the Education Commission 1964-66, NCERT New Delhi.

Kratz (1986). "The Encyclopedia of Education". chief Editor Lee. C. Deighton U.S. The Macmillan and the Freepress. vol. 9.

Kulandaivel, K. and Rao, T.R.S. (1968). "Qualities of good teachers and good students". (A Study of student rating) R.K. Mission Vidyalaya. Coimbatore.

Kumar, K. (1998). "Political Agenda of Education. A study of colonist and Nationals Ideas". Sage. New Delhi.

Lewin and Lockheed, M. (1993). "Operation Blackboard : Policy implementation in Indian Elementary Education". Ph.D. Thesis, University of Edinburgh. As found in Dyer's "Primary teachers and Policy Innovation in India. DPEP calling. Issue no. 15. New Delhi.

Lockheed, M. and Versppor (1993). "As found in Dyer's Primary teachers and Policy Innovation in India". DPEP calling. Issue no. 15. New Delhi. p. 13. Dyer, C. (1998). "Primary Teachers and Policy Innovation in India". As found in DPEP calling. Issue no. 15. new Delhi. p.p. 21-23.

Lockheed, M. and Verspoor, A. (1991). "Improving Primary Education in developing countries". The World Bank/ Oxford University Press, Newyork.

Luchins, A.S. and Luchins, E.H. (1966). " Learning, a complex ritualised social role". Psychological record 16: 177-187.

Makerenko (1951). "The road of life", role 3 p. 263. Mc.Graw Hills Book Comp. Newyork.

Malik, J.S. (1984). "A Comparative study of personality factors and Learning enviornments of successful and unsuccessful science teachers in selected schools of Rajasthan. Ph.D.Edn. M. Sukh U. As found in M.D. Buch. Fourth survey of Research in Education. 1984-89. NCER-New Delhi.

Mann, S.S. (1980). "Some correlates of success in teaching of secondary school teachers". Ph.D. Edn. Punjab U. As found in M.D. Buch. Third survey of Research in Education. 1979-83. NCERT-New Delhi.

Marja, Talvi and D. Bhaskara Rao, eds. (1996). "Educational Leadership and Social Changes". New Delhi : Discovery Publishing House.

Mathew, R. (1980). "Factorial Structure of Teaching Competencies among secondary school teachers". Ph.D.Edn. MSU. As found in M.D. Buch. Third survey of Research in Education. 1979-83. NCERT - New Delhi.

Mato, M.I. (1988). "Personality Characteristics Associated with Teacher effectivenees as seen through catell's 16 P.F. Test". Journal of the Institute of Educational Research. vol. 12 No. 2 p.1.

Mitchel, A. (1987). "what makes a good teacher? "Span p.p. 4-9.

Mutha, D.W. (1980). "An attitudinal and personality study of effective teachers". Ph.D. Psy.Jod.U. (In Buch 4th Survey Ed.)

NCTE (1998). "Primary Teachers and Policy Innovation in India. "Teacher Education in India." Edited by Dr. Bhaskara Rao, D. Discovery Publishing House. New Delhi.

Oliver and Shaver (1966). "As found in International Encyclopedia of Education, Research and studies." Edited by Torsten Husen and Postlethwaite. T.N. Pergamon press. vol.2. 1988.

Oxford Advanced Learner's Dictionary. Edited by Hornby. New Delhi. Oxford University press. 1996.

Piaget, J. (1952). "The origins of Intelligence in children". N.Y.W.W. Norton. As found in International Encyclopedia of Education. Pergamon Press. vol. 2.

Pillai, J.K. (1987). "Appraisal of Teacher effectiveness". New Frontiers in Education 17 No.4 Oct-Dec.

Ramakrishnaiah, D. and Digumarti bhaskara Rao (1999). "Job Satisfaction of College Teachers". New Delhi : Discovery Publishing House.

Rama Krishna. A. (1992) "Development of a scale for assessing the essential characteristics of secondary school teachers". M. Phil. Dissertation. Osmania University.

Rathaiah, Lavu and D. Bhaskara Rao (1996). "International Innovations in Education". New Delhi : Discovery Publishing House.

Rao, D. Bhaskara, ed. (1998). "Education for the 21st Century". New Delhi : Discovery Publishing House.

Rao, D. Bhaskara, ed. (1998). "District Primary Education Programme". New Delhi : Discovery Publishing House.

Rao, D. Bhaskara, ed. (1998). "Reforming School Education". New Delhi : Discovery Publishing House.

Reichard, G.A. (1938). "Social Life". In F. Boas (Ed.), General anthropology. Bostan: health, P.P. 409-418.

Reudiger, W.C. and Strayer, G.D. (1910). "The Qualities of meritorious teachers", Journal of Educational Psychology. p.p. 272-79.

Ryans, D.G. (1951). "A study of the extent of association of certain professional and personal data with judged effectiveness on teacher behaviour". Journal of Experimental Education. 20. p. 77.

Sah, A.K. (1991). "Systems Approach to Training and Development". Sterling Publishers ltd: New Delhi. p. 128.

Sansawal, D.N. and Jarial, G.S.(1979). "Personality differences among high and low creative teacher trainees". Dept. of Edn. Indore University.

Seagoe, M.V. (1945). Prognostic tests and teaching success". Journal of Educational research 39. p.p. 685-690.

Shannon, (1940). "A comparision of high successful teachers and average teachers at the time of their graduation from Indiana state teacher college". Educational administration and superision. 26: 43-53.

Sharma, M.L. (1979). "A study into the development of Teacher competencies of B.Ed. student teachers in the training colleges of Rajasthan", Ph.D.Edn. Raj University.

Sherry. *et.al.,* G.P. (1964). "A battery of Psychological tests for prediction of success in teaching". Ph.D.Edn. Agra University.

Simon, D.L. (1936). "Personality reasons for the dismissal of teachers in small schools". Journal of Educational research. vol. 29. p.p. 585-88.

Singh, S. (1979). "Relationship between teachers' personality and teaching success and behavioural changes in students". Ph.D. Edn. Udaipur U. As found in m.d. Buch. Third survey of Research in Education. 1979-83. NCERT - New Delhi.

Sinha, U. (1980). "The impact of Teacher Education Programme on the professional efficiency of the teachers". Ph.D. Edn. B.H.U. As found in M.D. Buch. third survey of Research in Education 1979-83. NCERT-New Delhi.

Swamy Ranganathananda (1993). "Role and Responsibility of Teachers in Building up Modern India". Bharathiya Vidya Bhavan. Coimbatore.

Thakur, T. (1976). "Who is a good teacher"A study based on the opinion of senior pupils. SIE. Assam.

UNESCO (1996). "Learning of those who teach". Towards a new paradigm of Teacher Education. Paris.

Valand, J.B. (1983). "A study of innovative process of teachers of primary teacher training Colleges in the state of Gujarat". Ph.D.Edn. SPU. As found in M.D. Buch. Third survey of Research in Education. 1979-83. NCERT - New Delhi.

Vijaya Bharathy, D. and Digumarti Bhaskara Rao (2000). "Educational Philosophies of Swami Vivekananda and John Dewey". New Delhi : APH Publishing Corporation.

Vena Kumari, B. and Digumarti Bhaskara Rao (1995). "Operation Blackboard". New Delhi : APH Publishing Corporation.

Venu Gopala Rao, K. and Digumarti Bhaskara Rao (2000). "Teacher Morale in Secondary Schools". New Delhi : Discovery Publishing House.

Vyas R.P. (1982). "Relationship of selected factors with the teaching success of prospective teachers of Rajasthan". Ph.D.Edn. Raj. U. As found in M.D. Buch. Third survey of Research in Education. 1979-83. NCERT-New Delhi.

World Bank (1990). "A World Bank Policy paper, Primary Education". Washington D.C.

APPENDIX-A

TEACHER COMPETENCIES OPINIONNAIRE

INSTRUCTIONS

This opinionnaire is meant for identification of teacher competencies. Hence, you are requested to kindly rate each of the characteristic under one of the columns of alternatives—Most Essential, Essential or Least Essential—given by placing a tick (3) mark as per your opinion.

Most Essential : The characteristic without which the teacher cannot become a competent person. Its absence makes the teacher incompetent.

Essential : The desirable characteristic that should present in a teacher.

Least Essential : The characteristic which is present in a teacher to some degree but its absence does not make the teacher incompetent.

PERSONAL DATA OF THE RESPONDENT

Name of the respondent

Designation

Educational qualifications

Teaching experience

Contributions made in the field of education

Signature of the respondent.

Teacher Competency Statments	Most Essential	Essential	Least Essential
The teacher			
1. should be in intimate contact with students and be friendly with them.	( )	( )	( )
2. Should realise the significance and relevance of teaching.	( )	( )	( )
3. Should be honest and sincere.	( )	( )	( )
4. should maintain sound relationships with community and public in general	( )	( )	( )
5. should endeavour to respect and take care of environment because he/she is a part of it.	( )	( )	( )
6. Should love his/her profession.	( )	( )	( )
7. should have sense of humour.	( )	( )	( )
8. must be unprejudiced and treate all students alike.	( )	( )	( )
9. should be everready to learn new things and constantly augment his/her knowledge base.	( )	( )	( )
10. must have emotional stability.	( )	( )	( )

(Contd...)

1	2	3	4
11. must use punishment and and reward wisely and sparingly.	( )	( )	( )
12. must be patient enough to help the pupils in studies.	( )	( )	( )
13. must descend to the level of students to enable them understand concepts better.	( )	( )	( )
14. should keep in view the individual differences of intellect in students and adapt suitable teaching techniques.	( )	( )	( )
15. should know the aims, goals and objectives of teaching the subject.	( )	( )	( )
16. must have the ability to understand the relationship between structure of the subject and its minimum levels of learning to develop the required competencies in student.	( )	( )	( )
17. should make students feel homely in school and that they have learnt something useful for their life.	( )	( )	( )
18. should plan his/her lesson well and know the skills of instructional management.	( )	( )	( )

(Contd...)

1	2	3	4
19. should evaluate students' performance from time to time and give appropriate work for the gifted and remedial work for the substandard.	( )	( )	( )
20. should encourage activity based learning among students.	( )	( )	( )
21. should identify and use environmental resources for organising different teching-learning activities according to priorities laid down for optimum utilisation at individual and at institutional level.	( )	( )	( )
22. the teacher should use teaching learning material as a means of meaningful interaction between the teacher and the taught and between pupils themselves to enable them work indepedently as well as collectively.	( )	( )	( )
23. should motivate pupils and incite interest in them to learn.	( )	( )	( )
24. should maintain discipline in classroom to facilitate smooth instruction.	( )	( )	( )

(Contd...)

1	2	3	4
25. must attend to various teacher training programmes and improve his teaching competencies.	( )	( )	( )
26. should develop leadership qualities in students.	( )	( )	( )
27. should stimulate, impress and inspire students not only by his teaching but by his/her personality also.	( )	( )	( )
28. should have scientific temper.	( )	( )	( )
29. should be prepared to sacrifice his/her privileges for the sake of his profession when demanded.	( )	( )	( )
30. should possess guidance and counselling skills to organise guidance and counselling sessions for the needy and the maladjusted students.	( )	( )	( )
31. must seek co-operation from the society and self-government institutions and ensure their participation to improve the quality of education	( )	( )	( )
32. should have self-confidence and develop it in students.	( )	( )	( )

(Contd...)

1	2	3	4
33. must take the help of colleagues and the Head of the institution to solve problems related to teaching social discipline and human relations and stream line personnel capabilities for effective maintenance of school.	( )	( )	( )
34. should identify the latent talents and aptitudes in students and try to draw out the best in them.	( )	( )	( )
35. must have verbal communicative skills as well as the non-verbal.	( )	( )	( )
36. should be aware of our cultural heritage and pass it on to students.	( )	( )	( )
37. should be a resourceful person.	( )	( )	( )
38. should be hard working.	( )	( )	( )
39. should help students develop their personality.	( )	( )	( )
40. should be cheerful and active.	( )	( )	( )
41. should effectively relate the subject matter in one area to other areas of the curriculum.	( )	( )	( )
42. should develop easy, original and innovative methods to aid instruction	( )	( )	( )

			(Contd…)
1	2	3	4
43. should communicate pupils' progress in various areas—cognitive, affective and psychomotor to parents by conducting meetings with them regularly.	( )	( )	( )
44. should develop moral values among students by giving striking examples from real life situations.	( )	( )	( )
45. must be noble minded and show extreme generosity in appraising the behaviour and motives of children.	( )	( )	( )
46. must be sympathetic and understanding in finding a solution to pupils personal and academic problems.	( )	( )	( )
47. must be adaptable to new situations and conditions and change his teaching to accord with the classroom requirements and procedures.	( )	( )	( )
48. must have consistent pattern in action and policy	( )	( )	( )
49. must have pleasant physical appearance.	( )	( )	( )
50. must have good reasoning and judgement skills.	( )	( )	( )

IDENTIFICATION OF NECESSARY COMPETENCIES

Necessary competencies are the skills required for efficient teaching and skills required for successful implementation of policies given by the Government from time to time. These necessary competencies include the most essential competencies and essential competencies discussed in the following pages.

"Most Essential competencies" are the characteristics without which the teacher cannot become a competent person. These are highly required skills for an individual entering teaching profession at primary level. "Essential Competencies" are desirable characteristics that should be possessed by an individual entering teaching profession at primary level.

In the following pages, data analysis for identifying 'most essential' competencies and for identifying 'essential' competencies have been given separately. They both together from the "Necessary Competencies" which are essential for the teachers for the teachers for efficient teaching.